CONTENTS
▼

8

To Jenny

ACKNOWLEDGMENTS

▼

We wish to thank the editorial, production, and marketing staffs of NavPress, especially Steve Webb, for their support of this project. Cathy Davis provided immensely valuable feedback as our consulting children's editor; *What's the Big Deal? Why God Cares About Sex* and *Facing the Facts: The Truth About Sex and You* especially benefited from her insights and editing skills. Our thanks go out to Sanna Baker and Carolyn Nystrom for reading and commenting on the early drafts of *The Story of Me*, and to Lisa, Mark, and Anna McMinn for reading and commenting on the early drafts of *What's the Big Deal?* Finally, our thanks to Carol Blauwkamp for help with typing parts of the early drafts of several of these books.

"GOD'S DESIGN FOR SEX" CHILDREN'S BOOK SERIES

▼

This book is one of a series designed to help parents shape their children's character, particularly in the area of sexuality. From their earliest years, our children are bombarded constantly with destructive and false messages about the nature of sexuality and the place of sexual intimacy in life through the media, discussions with their friends, and school sex-education programs. The result? Skyrocketing rates of teen sexual activity, pregnancy, abortion, sexually transmitted diseases, divorce, and devastated lives.

Our conclusion from studying this crisis, the nature of human sexuality, and most importantly, the Scriptures is that our God wants Christian parents to be the primary sex educators of their children. And if we are going to have a powerful impact, we must start early, working to lay a godly foundation of understanding of their sexuality before the twisted ideas of the world have a chance to take root. First messages are the most powerful; why wait until your child hears the wrong thing and then try to correct the misunderstanding? God made sexuality, and He made it as a beautiful gift; why not present it to our children the way God intended?

Our first book, *How and When to Tell Your Kids About Sex: A Lifelong Approach to Shaping Your Child's Sexual Character* (NavPress, 1993), was designed to provide parents with a comprehensive understanding of what they can do to shape their child's "sexual character." Some of our specific goals in that book were to:

- ☞ help you understand your role in shaping your child's views, attitudes, and beliefs about sexuality;
- ☞ help you understand and shape the building blocks of your child's character;
- ☞ clarify what God's view of our sexuality is;
- ☞ discuss how to explain and defend the traditional Christian view of sexual morality in these modern times;
- ☞ explore how you can most powerfully influence your child to make a decision for sexual abstinence (chastity); and
- ☞ equip you, the parent, to provide your child with the strengths necessary to stand by his or her commitments to traditional Christian morality.

In *How and When to Tell Your Kids About Sex* we provided numerous dialogues between parents and children at different ages, and offered many suggestions about how difficult subjects could be approached. Nevertheless, the most frequent comment we heard from parents who read our book was, "I really think you are right, but I don't think I can talk to my child that way. I wish there was something we could read with our children to get us started in discussing these matters." The books in this series are designed to meet that need.

For the sake of this children's book series, we have divided the years between birth and puberty into four time periods. We have made these periods overlap because there are differences in children's maturity levels that only you as a parent can know;

there are eight-year-olds who are more mature than some ten-year-olds, for example. The broad age ranges we have used are: three to five, five to eight, eight to eleven, and eleven to fourteen. We have written one book for each age range.

The first three of these four books are designed to be read *by parents to their children*. They are not, by themselves, meant to provide all of the information that kids need. They are to be *starting points* for you, the Christian parent, to discuss sexuality with your children in a manner appropriate to each age. They provide an anchor point for discussions, a jump-start to get discussions going. We suggest that you not simply hand these books to your child to read, because *it is how you as a parent handle the issue of sexuality that will have the greatest impact upon your child*. The fourth book is designed to be read by the child, now eleven to fourteen years in age, but we hope parents will also read the book and discuss its contents with the child.

Book One (Ages Three to Five): *The Story of Me*
Our most important task with a young child is to lay a spiritual *foundation* for the child's understanding of his or her sexuality. Book one helps you do that. It is vital that our children see their bodies and their sexuality (their "girl-ness" or "boy-ness") for what it is: a gift from God, a *marvelous* gift. They must see that God made their bodies on purpose, that God loves the human body (and the whole human person), and that God regards it as a work of divine art that in the beginning He called "very good" (Genesis 1:31). They must see that God loves women and men evenly; both are created in the image of God. Children must see not only their bodies, not only their existence as boys or girls, but also their sexual organs as a gift from God. They can begin to develop an appreciation for God's marvelous gift by understanding some of the basics of human reproduction, and so the growth of a child inside a mother's body and the birth process are discussed in this book. It is critical that children at this age begin to develop a trust for God's Law and see God

as a lawgiver who has the best interests of His people at heart. Finally, it is critical at this stage that children come to see families as God's intended framework for the nurture and love of children. We hope you will find *The Story of Me* a wonderful starting point for discussing sexuality with your young child.

Book Two (Ages Five to Eight): *Before I Was Born* (by Carolyn Nystrom)

Building upon the topics in book one, Carolyn Nystrom further emphasizes the creational goodness of our bodies, our existence as men and women, and our sexual organs. New topics are introduced as well. The book discusses growth and change in a boy's body as he becomes a man, and in a girl's body as she becomes a woman. Tactfully and directly, it explains the basic nature of sexual intercourse between a husband and wife. Undergirding this information is the foundation of Christian morality: that God wants sexual intercourse limited to marriage because it brings a husband and wife together in a way that honors God and helps build strong families. This foundation will be vitally important later in the life of your child.

It is not uncommon for parents to ask, "Do my kids really need to know about sexual intercourse this early?" The answer is yes. First, there is no good rationale for keeping kids ignorant about this basic area of life. We must remember that the Hebrew people, in and through whom God revealed His divine will, were farmers and ranchers among whom the breeding of animals was part of everyday life. Further, their culture was one with much less privacy than we have today. Homes were small, without glass for windows or stereos for background noise, and three or more generations commonly lived together. It was in the context of a society steeped in what we politely call "animal husbandry," a society with little privacy and definite "earthy" attitudes toward sexuality, that our Lord's will and rules about sexuality were revealed. We don't need to shelter our kids by keeping them "in the dark."

The second reason for telling your kids about sexual intercourse early is that positive, first messages are always the most powerful. Our children are exposed to the facts about sexual intercourse on the playgrounds of their schools and in the backyards of our neighborhoods. If we want to shape godly attitudes in our children about sex, why would we wait until they soak in the errors and misperceptions of the world and then try to change their attitudes? Why not instead build from the foundation up?

Book Three (Ages Eight to Eleven): *What's the Big Deal? Why God Cares About Sex*

This book attempts to do three things. First, it attempts to review and reinforce the messages of the first two books: the basics of sexual intercourse and the fundamental creational goodness of our sexuality.

Second, it attempts to continue the task of explicitly and deliberately building your child's understanding of why God intends sexual intercourse to be reserved for marriage.

Third, this book will attempt to help you begin the process of "inoculating" your child against the negative moral messages of the world. In *How and When to Tell Your Kids About Sex* we argue that Christian parents should *not* try to shelter their children from all of the destructive moral messages of the secular world. When we shelter them, we leave them naive and vulnerable, and we risk communicating that these negative messages are so powerful that Christians cannot deal with them. Too much sheltering will leave our children defenseless against the attacks they will receive from the world.

But neither should we just let our kids be inundated with destructive messages. The principle of inoculation suggests that we gently expose our kids to the contrary moral messages they will soon hear anyway. It should be in our *homes* that our kids first learn that many people in our world do not believe in reserving sex for marriage, as well as getting their first understanding of such problems as teenage pregnancy, AIDS, and so forth. But they should be exposed to these realities *for a vital purpose*, so that we parents can help build their defenses against these terrible problems of our culture. In doing so, we can strengthen their resolve to stand by the traditional Christian ethic and send them into the world prepared to defend their beliefs and choices.

Book Four (Ages Eleven to Fourteen): *Facing the Facts: The Truth About Sex and You*
Facing the Facts: The Truth About Sex and You will attempt again to build upon all that has come before, but will prepare your child for puberty in more depth. Your child is now old enough for more detailed information about the changes her or his body is about to go through, and about the adult body that is soon to be presented to her or him as a gift from God. Your child also needs to be reminded about God's view of sexuality, about His loving and beautiful intentions for how this gift should be used. The distorted ways in which our world views sex must be clearly labeled, and our children must be prepared to face views and beliefs contrary to those we are teaching them at home. We attempt to do all this while also talking about the many confusing feelings of puberty and early adolescence. We hope that our talking about these feelings will encourage loving conversation between you and your developing children as they go through this challenging period. This book is meant to be read by the child himself or herself, but we urge you to read it too, and then talk about it with your child.

All of these books were written as if dialogue were an ongoing reality between a child, his or her mother and father, and other siblings in the home. Yet in some homes only one parent is willing to talk about sex; in others only one of two parents is a Christian. Many Christian parents are not in intact, two-parent, "traditional" homes. We hope these books will be used by and be useful to single parents, grandparents who are the primary care-givers to a child or children, parents with just one child, adoptive or foster parents, and other families that do not fit the "traditional" mold. Obviously, use of these books by "nontraditional" families will require some special creativity and thought. But this is really no different from the challenges you face in talking about sex with your child in the first place. Sex education is hard when you do not have a partner who can share the other gender's perspective, when an absent partner is not a good role model, or when discussion of the topic raises painful memories and unresolved issues. We are concerned about these challenges but urge you *to press onward anyway*. The welfare of your child requires that you address the issues raised in these books. Better that they be addressed constructively and directly than left to fester unexplored.

Thank you for trusting us to help you in this great adventure of shaping your child's sexual character. We hope these books will be valuable tools in raising a new generation of faithful Christian young people who will have healthy, positive, accepting attitudes about their own sexuality; who will live confident, chaste lives as faithful witnesses to the work of Christ in their lives while they are single, and then fulfilled, loving, rewarding lives as spouses.

Remember that what you tell your child about sexuality is only part of the puzzle. How you live your lives as parents before your children will have the greatest impact upon them. Teenagers who have a close relationship with a parent are better prepared to resist sexual temptation and pressure than those who are disconnected from their parents; work on having a loving, caring, listening, supportive relationship with your teens. Encourage their own unique, independent relationship with the living God by family church attendance, by prayer and study of the Scriptures individually and as a family, and by the ways in which you live your everyday lives (Deuteronomy 6:1-9). Prayerfully send them out into the world, and always be available as a model of God's love, discipline, and forgiveness.

INTRODUCTION

In this book we have tried to tell the truth, God's truth, about sex and you. But you are old enough to know that many people disagree about "the truth" when it comes to sex. In the end *you*, the young person reading this book, will have to make up your mind about what *you* believe, how *you* will live, and what *you* will do. We hope that what we say in this book will help you make decisions in the area of sex that please God, and will make it easier for you to talk with your parents, your youth pastor, and perhaps even your friends about what you believe about this important area of life.

Some people your age are excited about growing up. Others are happy just as they are, and dread the changes that lie ahead. The truth is, growing up is hard *and* exciting.

You have always had your own unique personality. You have your own sense of humor, beliefs, favorite foods, favorite games, and ways to spend time alone. There is no one else exactly like you.

Being male or female is a very special part of what makes you *you*. Up until now you have been either a "man in the making" or a "woman under construction." But after the next few years of real change, no one will think of you as a child anymore. When you are an adult, how you think about your sexuality will have a big impact on who you are. Decisions about what you will and will not do with a boyfriend or girlfriend will have a profound effect on your future. And you are beginning to make up your mind about these things right now! Now is a good time to think through these things and begin to decide what sort of person you will be.

So, we invite you to join us as we try to share with you the truth about sex and you.

CHAPTER ONE

WHY IS GOD DOING THIS TO ME?

▼

Megan can't wait to grow up. As long as she can remember, she has looked forward to being an adult, to having the responsibilities and freedoms of an adult, to having a grownup body, and to moving on to whatever God has in store for her.

Chris, on the other hand, dreads growing up. He is happy just as he is. He loves his friends; he loves to play. Everything in his life feels like it's just the way it should be, and he sees no good reason why his childhood should end.

How do you feel about growing up? Are you excited or worried? Most of us have a mixture of good and bad feelings about growing up. It's hard! All of us mothers and fathers have been through the same feelings you are going through, though it's hard to remember, and even harder for us to talk about those feelings. Some of us asked the same question you may be asking: "Why is God doing this to me?" Good question. To answer it let's . . .

Start at the Beginning

Sex is God's idea. In the beginning, after God made everything else—sun, moon, stars, mountains and sky, plants, birds and fish, and all the other creatures—God made a man and a woman.

> So God created man in his own image,
>   in the image of God he created him;
>   male and female he created them.
>
> God blessed them and said to them, "Be fruitful and increase in number; fill the earth and subdue it. Rule over the fish of the sea and the birds of the air and over every living creature that moves on the ground." . . . God saw all that he had made, and it was very good. (Genesis 1:27-28,31)

At the end of every other day of Creation God looked out on what He made and saw that it was "good." But on the last day of Creation when He made man and woman God saw that it was "very good." The creation of man and woman was like frosting on the cake.

The Bible says that "the man and his wife were both naked, and they felt no shame" (Genesis 2:25). It's very important to realize what this means. God is happy with the way He designed people as sexual beings. God looked at Adam with his genitals, his ability to become a father, and everything that was unique about him as a man, and God was impressed with what He had made. God looked at Eve, with her genitals, her ability to carry a baby inside her body, her breasts to nourish that baby, and everything else that was unique about her as a woman, and

> **Genitals:** the male or female sexual organs that can be seen between the legs.

> **Sexual intercourse:** what many people call "having sex" or "making love."

God was very pleased with what He had made.

It was also God's idea that Adam and Eve would be able to have sexual intercourse as a man and wife, and God made their bodies so that this would be pleasurable and fun for them. It was God's design that they be able to have children because they had sexual intercourse. That was His plan for populating the earth.

God is happy that He made you a sexual being, with a unique brain, a unique body, unique genitals, and everything else that goes along with your being a young man or a young woman. One of God's main purposes for the changes He has ahead for you is to complete the work of transforming you from a child into an adult.

Adam Had It Made

You know the story. God made Adam first and put him into the Garden of Eden to take care of it. Even though Adam had the perfect job in the perfect place with a perfect relationship with God, God wanted things to be even better. He looked at Adam and said, "It is not good for the man to be alone. I will make a helper suitable for him."

God made each of us with a longing for a special person to share our lives with. While we are children, the love of our families can satisfy us. This is what families are meant to do. But God made us so that when we become adults we want something more. We want a special relationship that is just for us.

Genesis 2 says that after Adam looked around among all the animals and saw that there was no partner suitable for him, God made Eve and brought her to him. Adam was so excited about this wonderful gift from God that he cried out,

This is now bone of my bones
    and flesh of my flesh;
she shall be called "woman,"
    for she was taken out of man.

The writer of Genesis goes on to say, "For this reason a man will leave his father and mother and be united to his wife, and they will become one flesh."

"One flesh." What a beautiful way to describe the kind of relationship that God wants in a marriage blessed by Him. A powerful desire to be one flesh with another is planted deep in every person's heart. Even though our deepest desire is to know and love God, planted deep in our hearts is a desire for a special love relationship with another human being. God wanted it to be that way.

This is another reason why God is changing you, causing your body to grow from a child's body into an adult's body. Adults long to be united with a special person with whom they can have a lifelong love relationship. If you do not have those feelings yet, you will in the next three or four years. You will feel ready to fall in love with someone. Instead of sounding gross, the idea of being in love will sound great. And only when your body becomes an adult body can you have the kind of relationship where you will be "glued together" into one flesh with your husband or wife.

You Could Be a Model

Not everyone gets married. But if God blesses you with marriage, did you know that He has a marvelous purpose in mind for your marriage? The Bible teaches that marriages between Christians are meant to be models in this world of the way Christ loves His Church.

The joyful time when God welcomes His people home to Heaven is described as a wedding feast several times in the Bible. It's a joyous celebration when the husband-to-be (Jesus) finally gets to marry the bride that He loves (all of us who believe in Jesus). God wanted to put a model right on earth so everyone could see the wonderful love He has for His people. That's one reason why He made marriage.

God hopes that Christian husbands and wives will form loving, caring, committed relationships. If they do, the people who don't believe in Jesus will be able to look at these marriages and say, "Oh, now I get it. You're saying that the love that Jesus has for all of His people is like the love in that Christian marriage, just better and more perfect."

"For this reason a man will leave his father and mother and be united to his wife, and the two will become one flesh." This is a profound mystery—but I am talking about Christ and the church. (Ephesians 5:31-32)

Summing It Up

So, why is God doing this to you? Why does your body have to change into a grownup body? It's part of God's plan for you. He wants you to become the grownup, sexual person that He meant you to be. He wants to give you a way to meet that deep hunger you will feel for a special relationship with someone different from you who really loves you. He wants you to be a model here on earth of His love for His people, and He wants to make it possible for you to have children, if you choose to and are able to do so.

Put Away Your Flashlight

We all have mixed-up feelings about growing up, about our sexuality. Stan was given a small book about sex when he was about your age. He was dying to know more about sex. But he was ashamed and embarrassed for wanting to know—so embarrassed that he read the book only by flashlight at night when he was supposed to be asleep! You don't have to do that with this book. It's hard for parents and kids to talk together about sex. But even though it's hard, your parents bought you this book because they love you, and they want you to be able to understand this great gift of sexuality that God has given you. They can answer many questions you may have that we won't get to in this book.

CHAPTER TWO

HOW GOD MADE WOMEN AND MEN DIFFERENT

▼

Boys and girls, women and men, are more alike than different. Young men and women go through many of the same changes as their bodies shift from children's to adults' bodies. Whether you are a boy or a girl, you will go through a growth spurt. You will get taller, heavier, and stronger. You will develop more and darker hair on various parts of your body, especially on your arms and legs. You will begin to develop pubic hair (the curly hair that will grow just above your genitals). And many of you will develop what doctors call acne: the pimples, blackheads, and other skin problems caused by the excess oil your body will produce during these changes.

Okay, So What's Different?

The most obvious difference between men and women are their genitals. Many people use slang words to describe the genitals. We know one family that used the words *woo-woo* and *ding-ding* for the genitals. Perhaps some of you have

25

used the word *wiener* or *peter* for a man's penis. These kinds of words are not wrong, just silly. Slang can be confusing. We once knew a woman who grew up calling her genitals the "in-between-the-legs"!

But some slang is dirty or rude and should not be used. It takes what God made to be good and treats it as if it were evil. Some of the slang men use to talk about women's bodies is insulting, either because the words are ugly or because they imply that women's bodies are "to be used" by men. This is wrong.

Slang is often used out of habit ("That's what we called it in my family"). But slang is also often used because we are uncomfortable talking about our sexuality and feel nervous about using the correct words. In this book we will mostly use the words doctors use, unless those words are too complicated. Because our bodies were made by God, and sex is God's idea, we don't have to use slang.

What's Different About Women's Bodies?

Girls and women have three openings between their legs that go up into the inside of their bodies. One is exactly the same as men have, the anus. This is the opening that your bowel movements come out of. The anus is hidden in the crease between your buttocks in back.

Women have two other openings that go into the interior of their bodies. These openings are hidden in the crease between the labia between the woman's legs. When a young girl stands up in the tub to be rinsed off by her mom, all the mother can see of the girl's

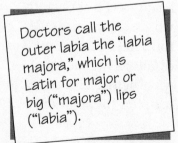

Doctors call the outer labia the "labia majora," which is Latin for major or big ("majora") lips ("labia").

genitals are the two labia and the fold or crease in between them. The labia are simply folds of skin that are soft because they are padded with extra muscle and fat like the lips on your face. Right above the place where the crease

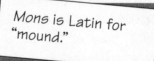

Outer labia

between the labia stops is what is called the mons. The mons is formed by part of the hipbone underneath the skin. This hipbone sticks out slightly, and has lots of muscles attached to it, giving it a soft feel.

> Mons is Latin for "mound."

The name doctors use for all of a girl's genital structures is "vulva," which means the mons, the labia, and the parts of the genitals between the labia that are not as readily seen. If your doctor ever talks about the vulva, she or he means this whole genital area. Some women just call this their genitals or "privates."

The structures between the labia usually cannot be seen except by deliberately spreading the legs and looking at them. Because the genitals of boys are on the outside, and because boys actually handle their genitals when they wash themselves or go to the bathroom, boys are more familiar with the way their genitals look than are girls. There is nothing

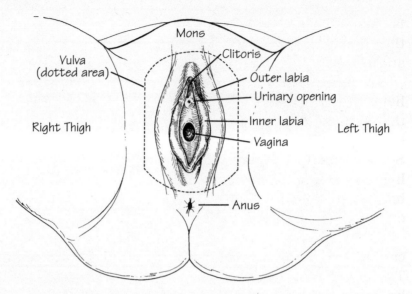

wrong with a girl looking at the marvelous way God made her. But to do so, she has to bend down and look or use a hand mirror to see how she is made.

God placed four structures between the outer labia. One is easy to see on some women and not so easy to see on others. This is the inner labia or lips, folds or looseness of the skin, that goes in from the outer labia toward the vagina. The inner labia or lips have

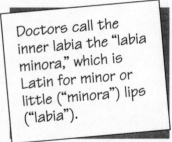

Doctors call the inner labia the "labia minora," which is Latin for minor or little ("minora") lips ("labia").

lots of nerve endings that make them very sensitive to touching. They seem to be one more gift from God to help a woman find pleasure in making love to her husband.

The woman's vagina is the easiest to see. The vagina is a tube that goes inside the body for three or four inches. The opening of the vagina looks like a small hole that opens into the inside of the woman's body. This opening is smaller in many girls who have not had sex because God made a piece of skin called the hymen to partially cover it. The hymen helps protect the inside of the vagina when a girl is young. When a woman has sex, this piece of skin is broken or stretched.

In some parts of the world the hymen is considered proof that the woman has never had sex before, but this is not a good test. Some girls are born with thick hymens and some are born with hardly any. Also, hymens on many girls naturally stretch or break when they do sports like track or gymnastics.

> The hymen is a circle of skin that makes the opening of the vagina smaller and helps protect a girl's vagina as she grows up.

The **vagina** is an interior tube made up of muscles covered with tissue like the tissue on the inside of your mouth. The vagina was made by God to do two things. One is to be the "birth canal" through which a baby comes out of the woman's womb and into the world. Most of the time the vagina is relaxed and somewhat closed, so it is hard to believe that this muscular tube can expand to let a baby's head and body pass through.

The other main purpose of the vagina is to take in the husband's penis during sexual intercourse. There are two special things about how God made the vagina for sexual intercourse. First, the vagina has a number of nerve endings that help it feel good when it is touched or rubbed. This is what happens when the husband's penis moves in the wife's vagina during sexual intercourse.

> During childbirth, a woman's vagina can stretch to the size of a baby's head, which is about the size of a small cantaloupe!

The other special thing that the vagina does is that it "lubricates." When a husband and wife have sexual intercourse, they move their bodies back and forth so that the husband's penis moves in and out of the woman's vagina. This would not feel good if the skin of his penis and her vagina were dry like the skin on your arm. So God made the woman's vagina so that when she feels full of love for her husband and is excited about being close to him and making love to him, her vagina automatically makes a watery **lubrication** that makes it very comfortable for her to have sexual intercourse.

This lubrication doesn't happen only when you are married, however. After a young woman has developed an adult body, she will sometimes feel her vagina get slightly wet. This can happen when she thinks about a boyfriend she is really attracted to, or sometimes after having dreams at night. This is perfectly normal and not something to be ashamed of or feel guilty about.

The third structure that can be seen between the labia, though with some difficulty, is the opening through which your urine comes out. This opening is called the **urinary opening**, and is located just above the vagina (toward the mons). Some girls think that their urine comes out through their vagina, but it doesn't. Urine comes from your bladder through a tube called the urethra and then out of this tiny urinary opening.

The final structure that is between a woman's labia is her **clitoris**. The clitoris is a small bump that is above the vagina and the urethra and below where the two labia come together. It is very sensitive to the touch. In fact, of all the parts of the woman's genitals, the clitoris has more nerve endings and is more wonderfully sensitive to touch than any other. It appears that God made the clitoris for only one purpose—to give a woman pleasure from being touched by her husband and by having sexual intercourse with him.

Women and men basically respond the same way to the pleasure of sex. Most married people say sex with their spouse brings them great joy. (Those who don't feel that way usually say it is because they don't love each other very much, because they can't talk about sex and don't understand each other, because they feel that sex is bad, or because something is wrong with one or both persons' bodies.) Husbands and wives both say touching each other feels wonderful. So does having sexual intercourse. If this pleasure continues, it can get stronger and stronger. If the couple keeps giving each other pleasure, both the husband and the wife can have an **orgasm**. An orgasm is when the pleasure of their bodies suddenly gets very strong, and the man or woman's body trembles a little all over. Most husbands and wives feel like stopping having sex when this happens, because they feel happy about the pleasure they had with the one they love.

What About Breasts?

When they are children, men's and women's breasts look alike. Both boys and girls have nipples that are slightly darker than the skin around them and breasts that are flat against the chest. But in adulthood men's breasts don't enlarge, while women's do. No matter what the size, women's breasts are made of the same parts. On the outside, a woman's breast is made of the same skin as the area around the breast with a nipple of darker skin. The ribs and muscles of a woman's

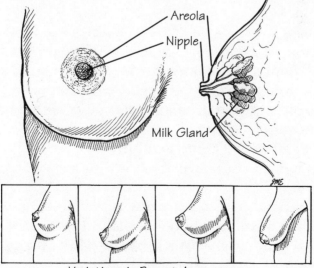

Variations in Breast Appearance

chest are the same as those of a man. The difference is what lies between the muscle of the woman's chest and the skin. The inside of her breast is formed of two parts: milk glands that connect to the woman's nipples through tiny tubes, and fatty tissue that makes her breasts soft. Women with small breasts have the same number of milk glands as women with large breasts. The only thing that makes one woman's breasts larger than another's is the amount of fatty tissue in the breast. The milk glands in a pregnant woman's breasts do not usually produce any milk until after she delivers a baby. There is no milk in the breasts of women who have never had a baby.

Women's bodies are a complex miracle! God made women in His image and blessed them with sexuality so they can enjoy a beautiful and exciting sexual relationship with their husbands, and also experience the joy of pregnancy, child-birth, and nursing a child. What a great idea God had!

So, What's Unique About Men's Bodies?

Men have two openings into the inside of their bodies that are located between their legs. Just like women, men have an anus for bowel movements located in the crease between the buttocks.

While a woman's vagina and clitoris are hidden from sight most of the time, a man's genitals are easy to see. Most obvious is the man's **penis**. A man's penis is made of soft, springy tissue, and has three main parts. The first is the shaft, which is the main part of the penis from where it comes out of the body to near the head or end. The skin on the shaft of the penis is a bit rough, sort of like skin on the man's arm or leg, except it doesn't usually have hair on it.

The second part of the penis is the foreskin. The fore-skin is like a continuation of loose skin from the shaft of the penis that covers over the head of the penis with an opening at the end.

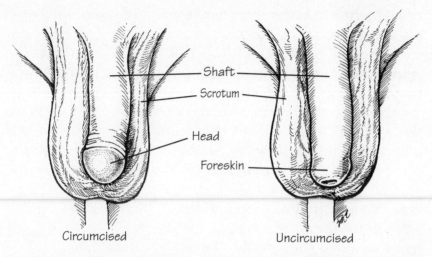

Circumcised   Uncircumcised

Some baby boys have most of their foreskin cut off while they are still in the hospital after being born. This is called **circumcision**. The head of the penis, instead of being hidden by a fold of extra skin from the foreskin, is now exposed all the time. Most boys born in America are circumcised, while most boys born in Europe are not; customs differ in other cultures. All Jewish baby boys are circumcised; this has been the practice of all Jews since the time of Abraham (read Genesis 17:10). Some early Christians argued that all Christians should be circumcised just like Jews, but the early Church, just a few years after the death and resurrection of Jesus, decided that this was not necessary (read about this in Acts 15). So some Christians are circumcised and some aren't! Doctors disagree as to which is healthier, but men who have been circumcised find it a little easier to keep the penis clean. Men who haven't been circumcised should pay careful attention to cleanliness by pulling back the foreskin when they bathe and washing around the head of the penis.

The third part of the man's penis is the head or "**glans**." The skin on the glans is different from the skin on the shaft; it is very smooth and sensitive. There is a hole or opening at the end of the man's penis through which he passes urine. This is the second opening to the inside of his body.

Underneath the penis there is a "bag" called the **scrotum**. Right underneath the skin of this bag is a layer of muscle. Inside the scrotum are the two **testes**. The testes cannot be seen from outside the body, but a boy can feel the testes when he touches his scrotum. They feel like two balls inside the sack, and that is why it is very common in slang terms to call a man's testes his "balls."

One of the jobs of the scrotum is to move and change automatically so the temperature of the testes inside it is just right. When a boy is very warm, the scrotum is loose and hangs down more, so

> The hormone that makes a boy into a man is called testosterone.

the testes inside can be cooler because they are farther away from his warm body. But when a boy is cold, the scrotum tightens up, pulling the testes inside up tight against the boy's warm body.

The testes have two important jobs. First, they produce the hormone called testosterone, which is a special chemical that changes a boy's body into a man's body and keeps him looking like a man throughout his life. A man who has had his testes removed slowly loses his beard and mass of muscles that usually go along with being an adult man. The other important thing that the testes do is produce the sperm that are essential to having children.

Men's bodies are also a complex miracle! Men are made in God's image, and their sexuality is a gift from God. Their bodies are made so they can enjoy sex every bit as much as their wives do. And their bodies were made so they can become fathers. Let's hear it for God's great ideas!

CHAPTER THREE

THE CHANGES AHEAD FOR GIRLS

▼

No Time Is the "Right" Time

Sometime between age nine and fifteen, and often around age eleven, a girl's body begins to become a woman's body. There is no right time for these changes to begin. Some girls' bodies start to change early, others late. Everyone is different. Girls who start going through these changes early often feel odd and may get teased by other kids. Sometimes girls who go through the changes late get teased too, especially when they change clothes in the locker room at school.

God has different timing for different people. There is nothing you can do to change your body's timing. If you are troubled because your body is changing earlier or later than your friends' bodies, please try not to worry about this or feel that there is something wrong with you. If your body is changing at the average time, you can help other girls by telling them there is nothing wrong with them and by helping them not to be hurt if they are teased.

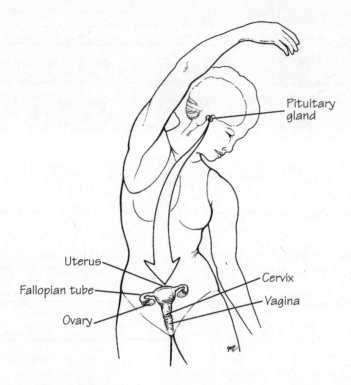

Pituitary gland

Uterus

Fallopian tube

Ovary

Cervix

Vagina

The Inside Story

We already talked about the sexual organs you can see from the outside: a girl's breasts, labia, vagina, clitoris, and so forth. Now let's talk about what is on the inside.

Remember that a woman's vagina goes up into her body for three or four inches. The vagina has an opening inside of it called the **cervix** that goes farther up inside the body. The cervix is like a tiny donut, with the hole in the middle squeezed closed. The cervix opens into the inside of the woman's **uterus**, or womb. The cervix is the very bottom part of the woman's uterus. The uterus is a muscular organ that provides a secure place for a baby to grow for nine months, and also brings in the life-giving air, food, and water that the baby needs. The uterus is powerful enough to squeeze the baby out of the woman's body when it's time to be born.

To find out how big your uterus is, squeeze your fist

closed and look at it. A woman's uterus is generally about the size of her closed fist. But when a woman is nine months pregnant and about to give birth, her uterus has expanded to almost the size of a small grocery bag, big enough to hold a baby!

At the top the uterus branches out into two tubes called the **fallopian tubes**, which go out from the uterus to the **ovaries**. The ovaries are very much like the man's testes and do two main

> The hormones that make a girl into a woman are estrogen and progesterone.

things: they produce eggs, and they produce the hormones that make a girl into a woman. The two ovaries are small and round, located up inside a woman's body on each side of a spot just below her bellybutton.

Puber . . . What?

Puberty is an awkward and funny word that means the time when a person's body is maturing sexually, usually lasting from one to two years. How does the body know when to start puberty? No

> Pu-ber-ty: the time during which a child's body is changed into an adult's body.

one is quite sure, but it is the "master gland" of the brain, the **pituitary gland**, that signals the girl's body to begin puberty. It sends chemical signals to other parts of the brain and to the ovaries to release their special chemicals, called hormones, which cause her body to begin changing.

What Happens First?

The first change most girls notice is that their breasts begin to develop. A young girl's nipple feels pretty much the same as the skin around the nipple. When breast growth begins, it starts right underneath her nipple so that she begins to feel a little "lump." For some girls the lump is very soft, and for others it is hard. Slowly, over a period of two to four years, the breasts begin to grow to their adult size. Like in the rest of the body, this growth can come in spurts.

Breast development occurs at different rates for different girls, and even at different rates in the same girl. For instance, many girls will notice one breast taking a couple of months to catch up with the development of the other. This can make finding a bra that fits well quite a challenge!

There is no such thing as a "normal" breast size. Angela wishes her breasts were larger, while Keesha wishes hers were smaller. Breast size varies as much as people size; some tiny people measure barely over four feet tall while giant people like professional basketball players tower over seven feet tall.

Is Bigger Really Better?

What does breast size mean? Does it make a difference? Breast size has absolutely nothing to do with a woman's ability to give milk to a baby through nursing. All women's breasts, no matter how small or large, have the same number of milk glands and the same capacity to give milk when they nurse a baby. Women's breasts differ in size because of the amount of fatty tissue in them. Women with bigger breasts simply have more fatty tissue in them.

Because a woman's breasts have sensitive nerve endings like her genitals do, most married women find it very pleasurable when their husbands touch their breasts. This is a normal part of making love and expressing affection in marriage. The size of a woman's breasts makes no difference in how much pleasure she gets from having her breasts touched. In fact, women who have very large breasts sometimes have less feeling in their breasts than women with average or smaller breasts.

One area where breast size can seem to make a difference is in being attractive to boys. Sadly, some men think big breasts are important for a woman to be attractive and will pay more attention to women with large breasts. Preferring women with one size of breast over another is sort of like preferring women with blue eyes to women with brown eyes. Both are beautiful. Since women can't do anything to increase or decrease the size of their breasts (don't believe those ads for exercises, creams, or pills; they don't work!), we urge you to not worry about breast size. Any young man who is using breast size as his main guide for whether you are attractive or not is not worth your time and energy!

About the time breast development starts, a girl's pubic hair begins to grow and her labia darkens slightly in color. At first pubic hair tends to be straight and a little thin. After several months, however, the hair gradually becomes more curly and thick. Women differ in terms of how thick their hair is in the genital area. Some have a very light growth of hair, while others have a lot of hair and may choose to remove some of it before wearing a swimsuit in public.

But That's Not All

While her breasts are beginning to develop, a girl's internal organs and genitals are beginning to change as well. The biggest changes happen so that when the right time comes, she will be able to get pregnant and carry a baby. And that's why the **menstrual period** is so important.

A young woman usually has her first menstrual period about twelve to eighteen months after her breasts begin to develop. Let's first talk about what a period is and then about what it's like and how to handle it.

Women with Rhythm

A woman goes through a rhythmic cycle about every twenty-eight days. Some women's cycles are longer (thirty-five or thirty-six days) while others are shorter (twenty-three or twenty-four days). Often, the first few cycles of young women just beginning to menstruate are irregular and unpredictable, but they usually become more regular as they get older.

For most women, the couple of days before menstruation begins is a time of mild discomfort. During this "premenstrual" time a woman might notice some mild cramps in her stomach, or be a little more tired than usual, and perhaps headachy. She might be more down or grumpy than usual. Every woman is different, and most women don't experience this time before their period as any big deal. Part of what will determine how you feel is your attitude toward your body. Women who feel good about themselves, about being a woman, and have a positive attitude seem to have fewer problems with this time before the period.

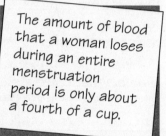

The amount of blood that a woman loses during an entire menstruation period is only about a fourth of a cup.

When menstruation begins, a small amount of blood

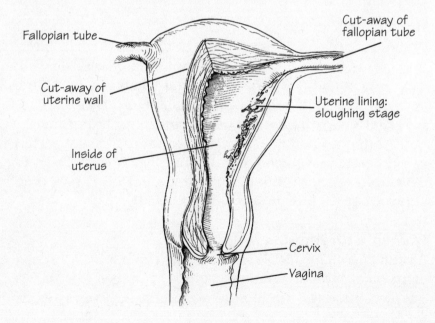

Fallopian tube

Cut-away of
fallopian tube

Cut-away of
uterine wall

Uterine lining:
sloughing stage

Inside of
uterus

Cervix

Vagina

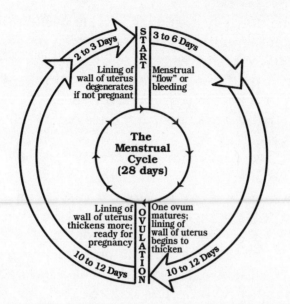

passes from the uterus through the cervix and vagina. The blood flow is typically heavier on the first and second days of the menstrual period, and then begins to slow down. Some women will have the blood flow for only three days, while others will have it for up to six days. A woman's period can change from time to time depending on how healthy she is, how much stress she is under, and other factors.

Why Have a Menstrual Period, Anyway?
The answer is tied to a woman's ability to get pregnant. Even when a woman is single and not having sexual intercourse, her body is still getting ready each month to carry a baby—to be pregnant.

During the eight or so days following the completion of a woman's menstrual period, her body is preparing an egg to be released by one of her ovaries. About the time her ovary releases the egg, about ten to twelve days after she stops menstruating, her body shifts gears rapidly and prepares the inside of her uterus to nourish a baby in case that egg gets fertilized and a child is conceived. That unborn baby will be nourished from the inside wall of the uterus from the mother's blood, so every month the wall of the uterus has to be made ready to nourish a baby. It does this by building up a lining that is very rich in blood and tissue, perfect for keeping the tiny baby alive. When the baby is a round ball of cells only a few days old, it will attach to the uterus.

A woman's uterus cannot be ready for pregnancy all the time. So after the ten to twelve days of getting the egg and ovaries ready, there is a ten- or twelve-day period of getting the lining of the uterus ready to have a baby attach to it. At the end of this time, if the woman's body has not detected that she is pregnant, she goes through a few days when the rich lining of blood and blood vessels, which her body so quickly built up just days before, now suddenly begins to fall apart.

After those few days, menstruation begins. Menstruation is the result of the uterus shedding the extra tissue, blood vessels, and blood that it had stored up in anticipation of pregnancy. So the flow that comes out of a woman's vagina is actually blood mixed with cells of tissue from the lining of the uterus.

What If I'm at School?
It can be a little nerve-racking to know that your first period could come at any time over several years! Even though you know that the first period usually occurs twelve to eighteen months after your breasts begin to develop, that's still a wide span of time to wait for something like this to happen.

Most girls don't feel confident that they will know what to do when their period starts. What if I'm in school? at a party? at the mall? at a sleep-over? alone at home? Most girls find out that they have started their periods when, after a couple days of not feeling quite right, they go to the bathroom and find some bloody flow on their panties or on the tissue when they wipe themselves.

If you have talked with your mother about your changing body, she can buy some sanitary napkins just for you that can be stored in the bathroom for when your period begins. All you have to do then is to change your panties, and begin wearing a sanitary napkin. Today, they are made to stick to your panties between the legs. Sanitary napkins are thin pads of cottony paper that soak up the menstrual flow and keep you clean. Most women's flow is heaviest during the first two days. During this time they change sanitary napkins several times a day. Later in the period, when there is much less blood flow, they might change less often.

Another way to take care of the menstrual flow is to use a tampon. A tampon is made of the same kind of absorbent material as the napkin, except that it is packed tighter, not in the shape of a pad but like a small tube the length of a two-inch pencil. A woman pushes the tampon gently into her vagina with either her finger or an applicator that comes with the tampons, and it absorbs the bleeding inside of her vagina instead of letting it flow out. The tampon comes with a string attached that hangs out of her vagina just slightly. Pulling on the string removes the tampon so she can throw it away. It's important to change tampons regularly. Some women who do not change them often enough develop health problems. For this reason, most women choose not to leave tampons in their vaginas while they sleep. The companies that make tampons say they have made changes that make them safer, but it is still better to be cautious.

Many girls are not comfortable using a tampon when they first begin having periods because they are not quite comfortable with menstruating and feel funny about pushing something into their vaginas. Some girls choose not to use tampons because they don't like the idea of putting something into their vaginas when they've never had sexual intercourse. Girls sometimes decide to use tampons because they want to do an activity like gymnastics or swimming that they can't do while wearing a sanitary napkin. Whether you use napkins or tampons is a personal choice that you can probably talk over with your mother.

If you think it through, you won't feel as nervous about your first period. If it occurs at school, you can go to the school nurse or to your teacher for help. If you have a man teacher you can simply say, "I would like to see the nurse (or talk to a woman office worker) because I don't feel well." A school nurse or woman counselor will have a supply of sanitary napkins on hand to help. If your first period comes when you are at a public place like a restaurant or mall, you will find that most public bathrooms have a sanitary-napkin dispenser. If nothing else, you can fold a bit of toilet tissue into the crotch of your panties until you can get a napkin. If you think ahead about what you will do when this happens, you will have no need for fear.

Many girls find it helpful to keep track of their periods on a calendar to get a better sense of what their regular cycle is going to be. As we said earlier, some women's cycles

		1 felt extra grumpy	2 headache and some mild cramps	3 began menstruating; took Tylenol	4 same	5 still menstruating, but not much
6 almost stopped	7 wore pad but no flow	8	9	10 had an upset stomach	11	12
13	14	15	16	17	18	19
20	21	22	23	24 had a headache	25 false alarm! Feel all better	26
27	28	29 a little headache, but not grumpy	30 started my period			

are shorter and some are longer. When your cycle becomes regular, you can predict fairly accurately when you might begin your period. This can help you plan when to carry napkins or tampons with you.

A Blessing or a Curse?

There is no one point when you stop being a child and become a woman. Some people with very mature bodies are as childish as any eight-year-old. And some fourteen-year-olds who have not gone through puberty yet can be quite mature. But having your first period is a clear signal that your body is becoming an adult body. This is the reason that many mothers celebrate the first period of their daughters. Women menstruate because of God's marvelous design for getting their bodies ready for pregnancy each month. Menstruation is a sign that you could get pregnant if you had sexual intercourse. You have made another big step toward adulthood. And that's something to be happy about!

But not all women feel good about having their periods. Have you ever heard a woman describe her period as "the curse"? She may be among those few who have tough physical symptoms with their period, like bad headaches or strong cramps. Even if your mother has these kinds of symptoms, that doesn't mean the same thing will happen to you. But if it does, you can talk to your mother and your doctor about how to make your period easier.

Some people feel bad about their period because bleeding just seems dirty. Others feel that because the opening of the vagina is just a few inches from the anus and right next to the urinary opening, the menstrual flow must be dirty in the same way as bowel movements and urine. But the vagina is very clean. God made the vagina to clean itself just as the skin on the inside of the mouth cleans itself. You have never washed the inside of your mouth with soap, but you don't worry about it being dirty. Nor is the menstrual flow "diseased" or "bad blood." It's no dirtier than the blood coming from a cut on your arm.

One reason that some women think of their period as "dirty" is that in the Old Testament the Jews were told by God (in the Law of Moses) that women who were in their period were "unclean" (for example, Leviticus 15:19-24). Does this mean that God is disgusted by menstruation, or that men should be disgusted with women who are menstruating? Absolutely not! Why then is this in the Bible? To understand this, you must first know that in the Bible the word *unclean* does not mean "dirty" the way we use that word today—full of germs and unhealthy to touch. And things that were unclean were not sinful.

God wanted His special people, the Jews, to understand that they were different from other people. To do this, God gave them His most important moral rules (like "Thou shalt not murder"), some important rules for how they should run their society (like rules for constructing buildings), and "ceremonial" rules that declared some things "unclean." Some of the things that were called unclean were part of normal life for the Jews—going to a funeral, having been in a war, menstruation, and even a man having a wet dream. Having these special rules made the Jews different from all other people. And since the time of the book of Acts (chapters 10 and 11), Christians haven't regarded the things the Old Testament calls "unclean" to be any problem for us. We aren't made special or different by our rules; we are different because we follow Jesus!

So, Celebrate Your Body!
Your body is a miracle—every part of it. You were designed and crafted exactly as God intended. You have a vagina, uterus, ovaries, breasts, and everything else that is special about women because God wanted it that way. He looked on Eve and said, "Very good!" He feels the same way about you.

CHAPTER FOUR

THE CHANGES AHEAD FOR BOYS

▼

If you are an eleven- or twelve-year-old boy, there is a good chance that your body has not yet begun the changes we call *puberty*—the time when a child's body is changing into an adult body. Most boys go through puberty between the ages of twelve and fourteen, while girls go through it between ages ten and thirteen.

At the end of puberty you won't be fully grown. But *sexually* your body will function like a man's body. If a thirteen-year-old boy has gone through puberty, he could become a father if he had sexual intercourse with a young woman.

Take Your Time

Just like young women, young men go through puberty at their own time. Some boys begin the process at age eleven or even younger, while others don't go through puberty until they're sixteen or seventeen. You might ask your parents when they went through puberty, because you will probably go through it about when either your father or your mother did.

47

The age you go through puberty has no effect on how healthy you are or whether you will have a satisfying marriage. Boys who go through puberty late, however, are sometimes teased by other boys at school. If you know boys who are going through puberty late, you can help protect and support them as they go through this process. Being called names can hurt and discourage a boy.

Signs of the Times

The first outward sign that a boy is beginning the process of puberty is usually the growth of pubic hair just above the penis. This hair often starts out thin and straight, but within six months or so usually becomes darker, thicker, and curlier. Most men also have some thinner hair growing on their scrotum.

Soon after a boy begins to grow pubic hair he will probably have a general growth spurt. During the puberty period, the penis and scrotum have a growth spurt of their own, growing a bit faster than the rest of the body and changing some in appearance. The skin on a boy's penis and scrotum looks a lot like the skin on the rest of his body, but as he becomes a man this skin gets a bit darker and rougher than the rest of his skin.

As the penis and scrotum begin to grow, young men often worry whether they are the "normal" size and look all right. Remember that the size of your penis changes a lot depending on how you are feeling, what the temperature is, and so forth. If you're cold, your scrotum tucks up against your body and your penis shrinks down to its smaller size. If you're warm and comfortable, the scrotum hangs loose and the penis is longer.

Wise About Size

There *are* differences in penis sizes, however. When young men shower together in school, they often glance around to see how they compare with other boys. It's obvious that

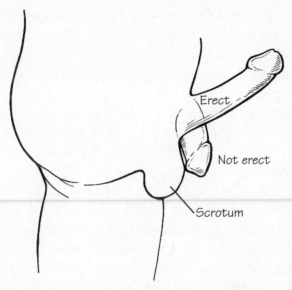

different young men have different penis sizes, depending upon whether they have gone through puberty or not. But it's true that some men just have larger penises than others.

You probably already know that an **erection** is when a young man's penis gets hard so that it sticks out from his body instead of hanging loosely as it normally does. When men have erections most of the differences in penis size disappear; the differences aren't that great.

In spite of what some boys whisper in jokes and locker-room bragging, the size of a man's penis doesn't seem to matter at all and has nothing to do with how much of a man he is, how strong or brave he is. It especially has nothing to do with how much fun and pleasure he will have with his wife when he is married. So the size of your penis is nothing to worry about.

How Do I Look?

Another concern that young men have is the way their scrotum looks. It's normal for one of the testes inside the scrotum to hang a little lower and a little more in front than the other.

During puberty boys begin to get more facial hair, starting with a few wispy whiskers at the corners of the mouth (the beginnings of a mustache) or on the tip of the chin. Sideburns usually begin to thicken and grow down farther than they used to. A man's beard comes in gradually. Some men are able to grow a full beard as early as age fifteen or sixteen, and others are unable to grow a thick beard even when they are forty. Men also begin to get more hair under their arms, on their arms and legs, and for some men, on their chests. There are big differences in how much hair men get in their beards, underarms, and chests, but this has nothing to do with how much of a man they are, or whether they will be good husbands later.

A young man's growth continues for some time after puberty. There are big differences in when men reach their full size. Some are at their full size by the time they are fifteen, but others continue growing into their early twenties. Before puberty, a boy can exercise all he wants and still not develop big muscles. After puberty, young men who exercise regularly can become stronger and their muscles will get bigger. Some men's bodies are built in such a way that exercise produces much bigger muscles than those of other men who exercise just as much. This is just a difference between individuals.

The Inside Story
We've been talking about the changes that are easy to see. But all this time changes have been happening on the inside as well.

It is the master gland at the bottom of the brain, the **pituitary**, that triggers the boy's body to begin the transformation into a man's body. The pituitary causes the boy's testes to begin making **testosterone**, the chemical that causes all of the major changes in his body. It is the testosterone, circulating through his blood, that causes all of the outside changes: the growth of body hair, muscles, and

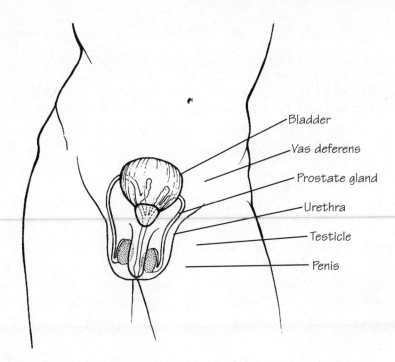

Bladder

Vas deferens

Prostate gland

Urethra

Testicle

Penis

greater height and weight. But testosterone also causes changes on the inside.

Your testes feel like hard balls, but are actually a densely packed group of tubes. On the inside of these tubes, sperm will be produced, while in the space between the tubes, the sexual hormone testosterone is produced. Testosterone is carried away from the testes by the blood vessels that nourish the testes. The many tubes inside each testicle (the singular form of testes) empty into a tiny tube that goes from inside your scrotal sack up inside your body. These two tubes, one from each testicle, go inside

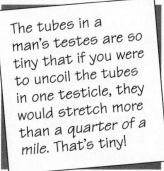

The tubes in a man's testes are so tiny that if you were to uncoil the tubes in one testicle, they would stretch more than a quarter of a mile. That's tiny!

your body and around your bladder (the muscle bag that holds your urine).

The **urethra** is the tube that goes from the bladder out

to the tip of your penis. Under the bladder, surrounding the urethra, is a gland called the prostate. It is inside the prostate that the two tubes from the testes connect into the urethra. So the urethra that opens at the end of a man's penis has three organs that empty into it—the bladder and two testes. The prostate is the place where these three all connect to the urethra.

The Sperm Game

At the same time that your testes start producing testosterone, they begin producing sperm. The average man produces 100 million sperm every twenty-four hours! Just to get an idea of that, imagine 70,000 people sitting in a football stadium for a game. To produce 100 million sperm in a day, a young man's testes must produce about as many sperm *every minute* as there are people in that football stadium!

Testosterone also starts the prostate and other small, previously inactive glands working. They begin to produce a fluid that is stored up by the young man's body and mixes with the sperm coming out of his body when he has an ejaculation.

What's All the Excitement About?

One of the biggest changes of puberty is that a young man begins to experience more sexual excitement, which usually causes more **erections**—when the penis gets harder and larger. Most boys have experienced erections at different times in their life. Erection is given different slang names, such as "getting a hard-on." Even baby boys get erections.

The skin of the penis has lots of nerves in it, especially on the head, or glans. These nerves are made by God in such a way that it feels good for the penis to be touched or rubbed. In this way, the head of the penis is just like a woman's clitoris; it was designed by God for pleasure!

One of the changes of puberty is that the pleasure a young man feels from his penis being touched increases. It feels much better than it ever did before. And when he feels pleasure from his penis being touched, he gets an erection. But that's not all.

After a boy goes through puberty, he naturally becomes more interested in girls and thinking about sex. Before, when he thought about sex, he didn't have any particular reaction. But when a young man thinks about sex, he often feels excited, and he begins to notice his penis having an erection.

Sometimes young men get erections for no obvious reason. They don't remember thinking about sex or anything in particular, and their penis hasn't been touched, but they suddenly find themselves getting an erection. This is just a normal part of growing up. It's very important for boys to realize that even if this happens at awkward times, like when you are sitting in class or while watching a movie, people generally can't tell that you have an erection and it's simply nothing to worry about.

How Does This Happen?

How does an erection occur? The penis has skin on the outside. The tube that passes urine, the urethra, runs down the center. The rest of the penis inside the skin and around the urethra is made up of a spongy, soft tissue that is different from any other in the man's body. When a man feels pleasure from his penis being touched or rubbed, God made his body to respond to that pleasure by automatically sending more blood to the penis. This blood gets packed into the spongy tissue of the penis so tightly that it makes the penis harder and bigger. It is sort of like blowing up a balloon. A balloon with no air in it is completely limp, but a balloon that has air tightly blown into it gets harder and stiffer. That is exactly what happens to a man's penis as it fills with blood. When it is not erect, a man's penis will usually be three or four inches long. When he gets an erection, his penis may be about twice that size.

Sometime during puberty a young man becomes capable for the first time in his life of having an **ejaculation**. From that time on, he is *capable* of becoming a father. He is certainly *not ready* to become a father or to have sex, but he is now producing sperm that can get a young woman pregnant.

When does an ejaculation occur? If a man gets more and more sexually excited, his excitement eventually builds to a peak. This happens in marriage when a couple have sexual intercourse. The man begins to have an erection when he is kissing and hugging his wife. If they then have sexual intercourse, the man finds this to be very exciting, and the pleasure builds up until he feels a burst of intense pleasure. This burst of intense pleasure is called an orgasm. At the same time as the orgasm his body spurts a mixture of sperm and other fluids out of his penis. That is an ejaculation.

How does this happen? When a young man's testes begin to produce sperm, the sperm are stored in the tube just outside of the testes. If the sperm are not ejaculated out of his body in a few days, they die and are reabsorbed by the body. They are replaced by freshly made sperm. Moments before the orgasm, the man's sperm move quickly from the testes through the tubes to the prostate. These tiny tubes are actually made of muscles that squeeze and release quickly all along their length, in just the same way that you squeeze toothpaste out of a tube. In the prostate the sperm mix with fluid from the prostate and other glands to make the milky white fluid, called semen, that will be ejected out of the penis. The semen enters the urethra, which uses the same kind of mus-

Semen: The milky white fluid that is a mixture of sperm and fluids from the prostate and other glands. Semen is spurted out of the penis when a man has an ejaculation.

cular squeezing and releasing to push (ejaculate) the semen from the prostate out through the end of the penis.

The amount of fluid that comes out of the urethra during an ejaculation is about a teaspoon or a little more. Inside that teaspoon of semen are 150 to 600 million sperm so tiny that if you were to remove these from the other fluids that make up the semen, there would be no noticeable decrease in the amount of fluid. Sperm can be seen only with a microscope.

How Can a Dream Be Wet?

Many boys experience their first ejaculation in their sleep. Doctors call this a nocturnal (or "night") emission, but most people just call it a wet dream. Wet dreams seem to occur naturally and are nothing to worry about or feel bad about. It's normal for boys to have erections three or four times every night, usually during a dream. In fact, it is common for men to wake up in the morning with an erection. Sometimes during a dream young men will get sexually excited and will have an orgasm with an ejaculation in their sleep. Sometimes this seems to happen with dreams that are about sex. A young man may wake up after having a wet dream and realize that he was dreaming about kissing a girlfriend or simply dreaming about talking with a girl that he really likes, or he may have been dreaming about sexual intercourse. Often, however, young men have wet dreams and can't remember their dreams having anything to do with sex. This too is perfectly normal.

Wet dreams are a normal part of growing up. You may have to change your underwear or wipe the semen off your sheets, but there is nothing abnormal or bad about having wet dreams.

Super Transformer

You are being transformed into an adult. Many changes have occurred in your body, and many more changes lie ahead in how you feel, how you will respond to women, and what is going to happen with your life. All of these changes are gifts from God. God wants you to use His gifts very carefully and bring Him glory. He wants you to have the best life possible.

CHAPTER FIVE

HOW DOES A WOMAN BECOME PREGNANT AND GIVE BIRTH?

▼

Becoming a parent can be one of the most wonderful events in your life. It is a miracle how a baby is conceived, develops inside the body of its mother, and emerges into this world as a tiny, new person.

But pregnancy and childbirth are not always such wonderful events. When a teenage girl gets pregnant outside of marriage, it changes the course of her whole life. Many unmarried women suddenly find that the man who whispered, "I love you, I'll always be with you, I want to share my life with you," suddenly drops her when he finds out she is pregnant. Many men not only do not marry the women they got pregnant, but also refuse to contribute any money or effort to care for the child, leading to legal and emotional battles.

How does someone become pregnant? Whether the pregnancy occurs in the right way, in the context of marriage, or in the wrong way, outside of marriage, the biological realities are amazing.

57

Now That's Planning Ahead!

While a man produces millions of new sperm every day of his life after he goes through puberty, a woman actually has all of the eggs her body will ever produce in her ovaries *before she is even born!* These eggs are preserved without change through her childhood years. Each egg is tiny, smaller than the period at the end of this sentence. But this is gigantic compared to the size of sperm produced by the man's body.

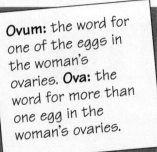

Ovum: the word for one of the eggs in the woman's ovaries. **Ova:** the word for more than one egg in the woman's ovaries.

The sperm and the ova are somewhat like seeds, but are different in one important way. An apple seed, for example, has everything necessary in it to grow an apple tree. But neither a human sperm nor an ovum has everything in itself to grow another human being. In fact, the most critical elements for growing a human being are the chromosomes that contain our genes, and the sperm and the egg each have exactly half of the chromosomes that are needed to create a new human being. The chromosomes of the sperm have to join with the chromosomes of the egg to start a new human person.

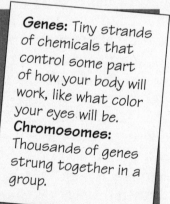

Genes: Tiny strands of chemicals that control some part of how your body will work, like what color your eyes will be. **Chromosomes:** Thousands of genes strung together in a group.

This is why every human being is physically unique—one of a kind. Human beings are formed from the chromosomes of a mother and the chromosomes of a father. These unique chromosomes combine to make a new pattern that has never been seen in the human race before. There has never been anyone exactly like you, and there will never again be anyone exactly like you.

A man's body is always producing sperm; his body is

always ready to help create a new baby. As a woman is finishing a menstrual period, her body is beginning to get ready for the possibility of pregnancy. Her hormones cause her ovaries to produce a mature ovum and to prepare it to be released. Several ova go through the process of maturing, but usu-

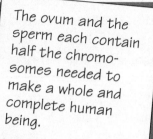

The ovum and the sperm each contain half the chromosomes needed to make a whole and complete human being.

ally only one is released and able to be fertilized by joining with a sperm. No one knows why one egg gets released and the others do not.

About ten to twelve days after a woman has stopped her menstrual flow, her ovary releases the mature egg, which is drawn into a fallopian tube. At the end of these tubes are fingerlike structures that wave gently over the ovary inside the woman's abdomen, creating a movement that draws the egg into the tube. The egg travels down the fallopian tube, a trip of only several inches but which takes several days. The mature egg that is released can be fertilized by a sperm

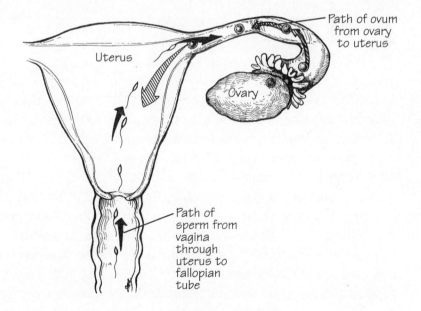

Path of ovum from ovary to uterus

Uterus

Ovary

Path of sperm from vagina through uterus to fallopian tube

for only about twenty-four hours. If a sperm does not meet and penetrate the egg during that twenty-four hours, the egg degenerates (or dies) and passes out of the woman's body with her menstrual flow at the end of that cycle. She will not become pregnant during this month.

A woman can only get pregnant during that one day of each month when her ovum has been released and is alive, ready to meet a sperm. But most women don't know for sure each month when they can get pregnant. Some women can tell that they are ovulating because they feel a wetness in their vagina. This wetness comes from their cervix (it's not the same as vaginal lubrication). Some of these women wear a panty-liner for a day or so while they are ovulating. Some women ovulate very early in their cycle, others ovulate late. There is really no time of the month when a person can say with absolute certainty that ovulation has not occurred and pregnancy is impossible.

> **Ovulation:** the time when a woman's ovary releases a mature egg that can then join with a sperm.

How Does Pregnancy Happen?

Remember that when a man and a woman have sexual intercourse, the man's penis goes inside the woman's vagina and soon the man ejaculates. When he ejaculates, between 150 and 600 million sperm come out of his penis into her vagina. Sperm are almost like tiny microscopic fish. They have a head and a tail that whips about to make them very efficient swimmers. Soon after they are out of the penis, they begin swimming.

Because they are so tiny, the journey from the woman's vagina up through the cervix, through the uterus, and through most of the fallopian tube to join with the ovum, or egg, is very long! Few sperm make it all the way. Of the average 200 million that start the journey, only a fraction make it out of the vagina and into the uterus. And only

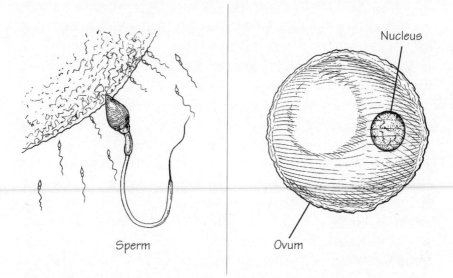

Nucleus

Sperm   Ovum

a fraction of those make it through the uterus to the open-ings of the fallopian tubes. Of those that make it this far, half go into the wrong fallopian tube. Only a few—probably only 50 to 200—of those that make it into the correct fallopian tube ever get close to the egg. You can see why so many sperm are needed.

But it only takes one sperm to **fertilize** an egg. The instant that sperm penetrates the outer layer of the egg, it becomes impossible for any other sperm to get inside the egg. Doctors say that the egg has been "fertilized" when the one sperm has gone into the egg. Once the head of the sperm is inside the egg it comes apart, releasing all of its chromosomes into the inside of the egg. These chro-mosomes from the man quickly join with the chromosomes of the woman. *At this moment, a baby has been conceived.*

Sexual intercourse is not the only way that pregnancy can happen. Any action that puts sperm in the woman's vagina or on her vulva can cause her to get pregnant. You may have heard how some couples who are having trouble get-ting pregnant will use **artificial insemination**. In artificial insemination, a woman gets pregnant not by having sexual intercourse, but by having the sperm of her husband placed inside her vagina or uterus by a doctor through a plastic tube.

Is Getting Pregnant Hard or Easy?

Women do not get pregnant every time they have sexual intercourse. As we said earlier, the egg can only be fertilized for about twenty-four hours before it begins to break apart and die. Sperm live between one and three days. This usually means that there are about three or four days each month when a woman can get pregnant. If she has sexual intercourse two or three days before she ovulates, her husband's sperm may be up in the fallopian tubes and still alive right when the egg is released. On the other hand, if the husband and wife have sexual intercourse just as the egg is released, the egg may stay alive just long enough for the fastest sperm to reach it, about twenty-four hours after it has been released. Sometimes, for reasons we don't understand, the sperm simply fail to reach the ovum. Sometimes, even though they reach the ovum, for mysterious reasons fertilization does not take place; either the sperm can't penetrate into the egg or they just miss it.

It may seem that it is hard to get pregnant. Many things can go wrong. Some couples who really want a baby find they have trouble getting pregnant. But it is much easier for most young women to get pregnant than many of us realize. Over one million teenage women get pregnant every year, and most of them did not mean to. Most women do not know with certainty when they ovulate, and we don't always know exactly how long the man's sperm might live. Some people try to prevent pregnancy by guessing when the woman is going to ovulate, but those guesses are often wrong.

People also try to prevent pregnancy in ways that are quite ridiculous. For instance, an old story says that if a woman gets up immediately after having sex and jumps up and down, this will shake most of the sperm out of her vagina and she will not get pregnant. This method does not work. Sperm begin swimming immediately when they get inside the vagina, and even if most of the semen shakes out by jumping up and down, enough sperm stay inside the vagina to easily get the woman pregnant. Some couples also think that if they stop having sexual intercourse before the man has an ejaculation there is no way the woman can get pregnant. This too is wrong because there is often a tiny drop of fluid that comes from a man's penis even before he ejaculates, and this tiny drop sometimes contains live sperm. It only takes one sperm to get a woman pregnant.

How Do Twins Happen?

There are two types of multiple births. One happens when only one egg is released and gets fertilized. The other occurs when the woman releases more than one egg and more than one get fertilized.

"Identical" twins start off the same way all single births do: the woman releases one egg, which is fertilized by one sperm. But something happens very early, possibly even before the developing baby attaches to the inside wall of the uterus. For unknown reasons the fertilized egg, which begins to divide into smaller and more cells, does something that usually doesn't happen. It splits completely in two and begins to develop as two babies rather than one. These

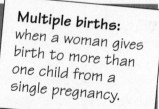

Multiple births: when a woman gives birth to more than one child from a single pregnancy.

two babies started from the same single cell, and so have the exact same chromosomes. Because it's the chromosomes that cause us to have certain physical characteristics, these twins will look just alike.

If the woman releases two (or even three or four) eggs and if each joins with a different sperm, the woman will have twins (or triplets or quadruplets) that are not identical, called "fraternal" twins. Because each fraternal twin comes from a different egg and different sperm, they look no more alike than do other brothers and sisters in the family. They have no reason to look identical, because their chromosomes are just as different as a brother's and sister's born five years apart.

Nothing can be done to cause a woman to have identical twins, and no one is sure why it happens. Fraternal pregnancies appear to happen because some women's bodies just release more than one egg on a regular basis. We do know that some drugs that doctors give women who are having trouble getting pregnant cause their ovaries to release multiple eggs, so women on these drugs are more likely to have multiple births than other women.

How Does a Woman Know She's Pregnant?

The first sign most women have that they are pregnant is that they don't have their next period when they expected it. The purpose of the menstrual cycle is for the woman's uterus to get ready to become pregnant. Once she is pregnant, there is no need to let the blood and tissue go from the inside of the uterus. In fact, the developing baby needs the extra blood flow from the mother to give it the oxygen and food that it needs to grow. So, when women are pregnant, they don't normally have any bleeding or menstrual flow.

Just because a woman misses her period doesn't mean she is pregnant. Sometimes women don't have their menstrual flow at the normal time because they have been sick, or because they have been very upset and tired. There are lots of reasons for a woman to be late or to skip a menstrual cycle.

About two weeks after she would have normally had her period, some unique chemicals appear in a woman's urine and blood that, when tested, will definitely show whether or not she is pregnant. About the same time, if a woman is pregnant, she begins to experience some other signs such as mild nausea. Because most women have this sick-to-their-stomach feeling more frequently in the morning, it's called "morning sickness." This nausea usually stops after a few weeks.

The Rest of the Story

After the egg is fertilized, it continues down the fallopian tube for another day or two until it comes into the uterus. At first it is only one cell with a mixture of chromosomes from the woman and the man. Then it begins to divide. One cell splits into two, two into four, and on and on, slowly at first. But the dividing soon picks up speed and this begins the remarkable growth of the baby. Within a day or two, it has become a compact ball of cells.

The next critical stage is for the baby to attach or stick to the side of the uterus. This is called **implantation**. If the tiny ball of cells that forms the baby implants, it is likely to grow and be born a healthy, whole baby. If it doesn't implant, but continues down the uterus and through the cervix, it will die from lack of nutrition and simply be passed out of the body. Usually when this happens the woman never knew that her egg was fertilized and a new life conceived. There is nothing that can be done about this, and no one knows why some babies implant and others don't.

If the baby implants, it continues to develop rapidly. With nourishment that it receives from the uterine wall, it now begins to grow and divide. At first the dividing cells all look the same. But soon a tiny brain begins to form, followed by a tiny spinal cord. The internal organs start to form: heart, lungs, and liver. Arm buds, leg buds, and a tail begin to form. The tail disappears later, while your other parts grow and develop rapidly.

At the time of this early growth a placenta is formed right where the baby connects to the wall of the uterus. The **placenta** is an organ with lots of blood vessels in it that takes oxygen and food from the blood of the mother in the wall of her uterus and absorbs them into the blood of the baby. From the placenta, the **umbilical cord** carries these nutrients into the baby's body. The umbilical cord connects to the baby's body at the point we call our navel, or bellybutton.

Your navel is the scar that was left when your umbilical cord dried up and fell off after you were born.

You Could Be as Big as an Elephant!

The rapid development of the baby is incredible. If we grew as fast *after* we were born as we did while we were in our mother's uterus, we would be the size of elephants by the time we reached four or five years old. We grow from one cell tinier than a grain of sand to an average of seven or eight pounds and about twenty-one inches long within the space of nine months. Now *that* is astounding growth!

For reasons that are not well understood, some babies die after they begin to grow in the mother's uterus. This is called a **miscarriage**. Research suggests that babies who die before they are born often have something seriously wrong with their bodies, something that would make it impossible for them to live. But no one knows why most miscarriages occur.

Is There Enough Room?

How does a pregnant woman's body make room for a baby? Her uterus, normally the size of her closed fist, grows large enough to hold even a nine-or ten-pound baby. So to make room for this baby, her other internal organs get pressed and pushed out of the way. Toward the end of their pregnancies most women find that they have to go to the bathroom much more often because their bladders are pressed and not able to hold as much urine as they used to. Many pregnant women find that they have to eat several small meals instead of three regular meals during the day because their stomachs and intestines are so compressed that they can't hold as much food as they used to.

Pregnant women often experience muscle aches because their bodies are not used to carrying the extra weight that comes with pregnancy. In addition to the weight of a seven- to nine-pound baby, most women gain an additional ten to twenty-five pounds because of other changes in their bodies. Toward the end of their pregnancies, one change that always occurs is in their breasts. Women's breasts usually grow in size as the milk ducts expand and get ready for milk production. That milk production is called **lactation**.

It Sounds like a Lot of Work

Nobody knows what begins the process of labor, but after about nine months, the woman begins to experience labor pains. This is because the uterus, which is made

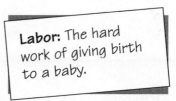

Labor: The hard work of giving birth to a baby.

of sheets of muscle, is squeezing and forcing the baby down lower. The strongest muscles in the uterus are at the top, and they begin to contract to push the baby out through the cervix and vagina.

For the average woman, labor lasts about fourteen hours for the first child and shorter for other children. During those fourteen hours, the cervix, which is normally closed, is slowly forced open. God made women's bodies so that their hips are able to stretch and flex so the baby can go through the circle of bone at the base of the hips and on through the cervix and out of her vagina. If the entire birth process takes fourteen hours, the first thirteen are required just to get the hips and cervix to open large enough for the baby's head to come through. Once they are open enough, the birth proceeds very rapidly.

The woman begins to push hard to get the baby through the cervix and through the vagina. The vagina, which is normally quite a small tube, is made by God to stretch

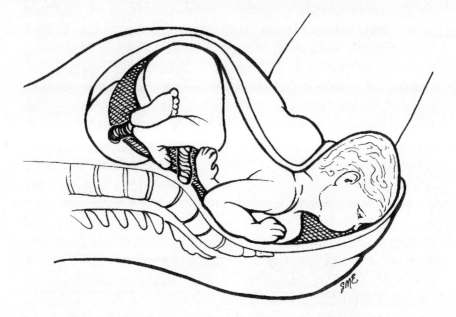

during the birth process to let the baby come through. The normal way of delivery is for the baby to come out head-first. As the woman pushes, the baby's head, which is specially designed to force the cervix open and to pass through the vagina, appears in the outside world for the first time. The doctor cuts the umbilical cord, and soon after the baby comes out of the woman's vagina, the rest of the umbilical cord and placenta comes out as well.

Childbirth hurts. Don't let anyone tell you otherwise. But a woman's body is very resilient, designed by God just for this purpose. After giving birth to a child, a woman is extremely tired and overwhelmed with how much pain and work it was, but she is also overjoyed with the marvelous gift of her baby. She is able to hold it and be with it right away.

It takes a number of months for a woman's body to return to normal. The uterus, which was so stretched out of shape, slowly returns to normal. The woman usually loses much of the extra weight she gained. Her hips return to their firm condition, and most of the other changes of her body go back to normal. Her vagina and cervix heal from the stretching they went through, and usually go back to about the same size they were before.

Not all babies can be born through the vagina. Sometimes when babies are not in the head-down position but are bottom down, doctors decide it is too big a risk to give birth to the baby through the vagina and so deliver it through an operation. Doctors also sometimes deliver babies through operations when a woman's passageway through her hips is not big enough to let a big baby be born, or because they are afraid that a baby may not be strong enough to survive the difficult process of being pushed through the vagina.

This operation is called a **Caesarean section**. Doctors give the mother an anesthetic that makes her numb to pain, and then they make a cut right above the woman's pubic hair through the muscle to the woman's uterus. They carefully cut through the wall of the uterus and remove the baby through this incision. Then they sew the wall of the uterus, the muscles of the abdomen, and the skin back together. The woman has a healthy baby, even though the baby was not delivered through the vagina.

Getting the Right Start

Just as God made women's bodies to care for babies before birth, He made women's breasts for feeding their babies after they are born. During the first few days after birth, a mother's breasts give out a substance called **colostrum**. Colostrum has some food value, but this watery, yellowish liquid mainly acts like medicine for the baby, helping it resist diseases and infections that might threaten its life in its first few weeks out in the world.

But soon, within several days, the mother's milk begins to be produced; this is called lactation. The milk that is made in a human mother's breasts is the perfect food for the baby. Babies would be malnourished and grow up abnormal if they were fed nothing but cow's milk. The mother eats more than she normally would during this time because her body uses up extra food making the milk. The milk builds up in her breasts over two to three hours. Then when the baby cries or begins to suckle on her breast, she experiences a "letdown reflex" when the milk is released from the milk glands to flow out of her nipples. For many different reasons, some women choose to feed their babies specially designed baby formula rather than nurse them with their own breast milk.

Most babies live on nothing but their mothers' milk (or their bottle formula) for five to eight months before mothers begin to give them other kinds of simple foods they can digest. Some babies will stop nursing soon after they begin to eat other foods, while other children continue to nurse, though much less than they used to, for months and even years after they begin to eat other foods.

What a miracle that any of us are born! What a gift God gave us in our sexuality and ability to have children. What does God say about how we should handle this beautiful gift? That's our next subject.

CHAPTER SIX

WHY SAVE SEX FOR MARRIAGE?

▼

Sometimes it seems like everyone is having sex. Some kids in high school talk as if they have sex all the time. Not many kids admit to being a "virgin," the word for anybody who has not had sexual intercourse yet. In many groups "virgin" is used as an insult instead of a virtue. Characters on television and movies will often move quickly from their first meeting to a "bedroom scene." In many school sex-education classes, there is much more talk about using birth control when you *do* have sex than about choosing *not* to have sex. A teenager who chooses not to have sex can feel a little lonely!

People will try to convince you that the Christian way of saving sexual intercourse for marriage is stupid. They will tell you things like:

☞ "Sex is the very best way to express affection and love—if you really love someone, you will have sex with him or her."

71

☞ "You must have sex to be a mature, normal, and grownup person."

☞ "You simply must have sex—the desire for sex is so strong it cannot be resisted."

☞ "It's important to try sex before you get married to make sure you are 'sexually compatible.'"

☞ "It is important to have sex to practice for marriage."

☞ "Sex is *always* good."

It's important that you know that every single one of these arguments is terribly wrong. But . . .

If They're Wrong, What's Right?

One of the most important things for you to do is to decide what you believe about sex. Beyond just the *facts* about our bodies, which we have talked about in the last four chapters, what do you believe sex is for and how should it be used?

Christians believe that our bodies are a good gift from God. He intentionally made the sexual parts of our bodies to be wonderfully sensitive. He gave us the capacity for great pleasure. Of course, nonChristians believe that our bodies are good and able to give us great pleasure, also. But one way in which we Christians are different from people who don't believe in God is that we believe our bodies are a *gift* from God.

We treat gifts differently than we treat things that we have made or bought. If you work to earn money and then use that money to buy a toy, you may feel you can do anything you want with it, maybe even break it or destroy it. But we usually don't feel that way about gifts. We see a gift as an expression of love and caring from another person. And it's right to feel that way about the gift of sex. It's important to think about how God wants us to use that gift.

We adults feel a special longing in our hearts for someone special to love and be loved by for our entire lives. God made sexual intercourse to be a special "glue" that helps hold two people together for a lifetime of marriage. The Bible teaches that when two people have sex, they become "one flesh." Nobody fully understands this mystery. God does not give us the answer in the Bible. But even though it's a mystery, it's true: sex was meant to glue two people together for life.

This doesn't mean, however, that any two people who have sex are married. A person who's had sex with two or ten or more people is not married to all of those people. And persons who have sex as teenagers should not feel that they must marry their sexual partner. Marriages that start out this way often end in divorce and disaster. The Bible teaches us just how special this gift of sexual intercourse is and why it's worth waiting for.

When a husband and wife have sexual intercourse, they completely share their bodies with each other. If they truly love each other and can talk and share with each other, then having sexual intercourse can truly be what people call it: "making love." The couple will have sex because they love each other, and they will love each other more because they have sex.

The reasons to save sexual intercourse until you are married are . . .

Reason 1: To Be Safe

You've probably heard people talk about the importance of "safe sex." That's because sex can be very dangerous. There are two big *physical* dangers of sex outside of marriage. The first is the risk of sexually transmitted diseases (STDs) like gonorrhea, syphilis, chlamydia, genital herpes, viral hepatitis, genital warts, and others. One of these STDs, syphilis, can kill you when left untreated. But all have serious consequences. Besides being very uncomfortable, several of them can damage a woman's body so that she can *never* get pregnant and have babies. Some can cause pain whenever you try to have sex.

The worst STD, the one that cannot be cured and almost always results in death, is HIV, the infection that results in AIDS. AIDS is the final stage that comes from being infected by the HIV, and it is in the AIDS stage that people die.

All sexually transmitted diseases are passed by a person with the germs in his or her body to the person he or she has sex with. There is an old saying that when you have sex with someone, you are having sex with *every other person your partner ever had sex with*. What does this mean? Let's say you know a sixteen-year-old girl who has had sex before, and she chooses to have sex with her eighteen-year-old boyfriend because she really feels "in love." Maybe he has had sex with three other women before your friend. Let's suppose that one of those other women had sex with six different men. If one of those six men had syphilis or gonorrhea, he probably passed it on to that girl, who in turn passed it to her new boyfriend, who is now likely to pass that disease to your friend. This is the way sexually transmitted diseases are passed.

You are probably asking, "How can I be sure that I never get one

> Sexually transmitted diseases, or STDs, are diseases that are spread by people having sex. They are diseases whose germs are either concentrated in a man's semen or woman's vaginal lubrication, or which are most easily spread through the delicate tissues of the man and woman's genitals.

> STDs are more common today than at any other time in history. Several studies have shown that over one-third of all college women have already had at least one STD by the time they are twenty-one years old!

> **HIV:** human immunodeficiency virus; **AIDS:** acquired immunodeficiency syndrome.

of these sexually transmitted diseases?" The answer is simple. If you save sex for the person you marry, and that person also saves sex for marriage with you, then neither of you ever has to worry about having a sexually transmitted disease.

There's another physical danger of sexual intercourse. It's almost always possible for the woman to get pregnant when a couple has sexual intercourse. Many medical problems result from a woman getting pregnant when she is a teenager. Babies born to teenage mothers are more likely to be born underweight or premature. A teenage mother is more likely to be hospitalized or have other medical problems as a result of her pregnancy.

The physical risks aren't the only concern. A young woman who chooses to have an abortion will have to go through life knowing that she let a doctor kill the baby inside her body because she didn't want that baby. If she chooses to have the baby, her friendships may change when friends pull away from her because they don't want to share that experience with her and can't relate to what she is going through. Teenage mothers are more likely to drop out of school, and to live in poverty because they can't get a job. Teenage fathers are less likely to help with the baby or help support the mother with money than are married, mature fathers. There is lots of research that shows that children who grow up with only one parent are not as happy as children who grow up in families with two parents. The children do not do as well in school, get into trouble with the police more, and are more likely to have children of their own while they are still teenagers than are children whose parents are married and both active in raising their children.

About 1 million teenage women get pregnant each year. About half of those, about 500,000 young women under twenty, choose to have their baby aborted each year.

What About Condoms?

Many people will say that while sex outside of marriage is never completely safe, it can at least be made "safer" by using a condom. There are condom advertisements on television, posters, and everywhere today. What are condoms?

A condom is shaped like a balloon and most are made of a substance called latex, which is like rubber. The condom rolls over a man's penis before the couple has sexual intercourse, and they are supposed to leave it on the whole time that they have sexual intercourse. The condom does two things when it works right. It catches the man's semen when he ejaculates. Since the semen does not go into the woman's body, she shouldn't get pregnant. The condom also prevents the man's skin and semen from touching the inside of the woman's body and her vagina, and that helps prevent germs from crossing from his body to hers or from her body to his.

Condoms do make sex physically safer. But how safe do they make it? Imagine you have a seven-year-old brother, and you live near a big highway. One day when you are baby-sitting your brother, he wants to play on the highway. You know that letting him play on the highway would be deadly. Would you let him play there? Of course not. But suppose he asks that you let him play on the shoulder of the road where the cars don't usually drive. Is that a good idea? Suppose he asks to play on the hill right next to the highway where he could accidentally roll down the hill onto the shoulder of the road. Would this be all right because it's safer?

When people have sex outside of marriage, sex is physically safer if they use a condom than if they don't. But they are still taking risks. People who use condoms don't get pregnant as often, but they do get pregnant. They do not get diseases as often, but they do get diseases, including AIDS. This is partly because condoms don't work perfectly.

Sometimes they break. Sometimes they have tiny holes that can't be seen but are big enough for germs and semen to get through. Also, condoms often fail to work because many people, especially teenagers, don't use them correctly. And there are some sexually transmitted diseases that condoms do not stop.

The physical consequences of sex outside of marriage, including the possibility of getting pregnant or getting a disease, are truly scary. One reason to save sex for marriage is to stop these bad things from happening to you. But this is not the most important reason not to have sex before you are married.

Reason 2: To Obey God to Show Him You Love Him

A second and vital reason for not having sex outside of marriage is because God does not want you to. Jesus once said, "If you love me, you will obey what I command." God wants us to show our love for Him by the way we live our lives. We can honor God with our hearts and minds by believing and trusting in Him. And we can honor God with our bodies by using them to do good and not the things God doesn't approve of. The Bible teaches that when we save sexual intercourse for marriage, we are honoring God with our bodies. Obeying is a way of showing who we love. We can show God who we really love by what we do with our bodies.

The physical dangers of sex we talked about in reason 1 are only part of the story. Sex before

> Jesus answered, "I am the way and the truth and the life. No one comes to the Father except through me. . . . If you love me, you will obey what I command. . . . If anyone loves me, he will obey my teaching. My Father will love him, and we will come to him and make our home with him. He who does not love me will not obey my teaching. These words you hear are not my own; they belong to the Father who sent me." (John 14:6,15,23-24)

marriage also puts you in spiritual danger. Why? Because the Bible teaches that obeying God helps us grow close to Him, and disobeying God often causes us to drift away from Him and our love for Him to grow cold. Young people who misuse the gift of their sexuality by having sex before they are married are not only taking physical risks; they are also gambling with their relationship with God.

Reason 3: Sex Is Meant for a Special Purpose—Unity ~~Babies~~

Sex was made to be a special bond between a husband and wife in marriage. Remember that Genesis 2:24 verse? "For this reason a man will leave his father and mother and be united to his wife, and they will become one flesh."

Sexual intercourse unites two people. It bonds them, glues them together, joins them in some mysterious way that the Bible itself does not explain. Sex is a life-uniting act. It was meant to be used as a special gift in marriage, to help bond two people together for life. If we use it any other way, such as to have fun or prove that we are a real man or woman, we are doing the wrong thing with this gift.

Sex outside of marriage not only can hurt us physically and

> We know that we have come to know him if we obey his commands. The man who says, "I know him," but does not do what he commands is a liar, and the truth is not in him. But if anyone obeys his word, God's love is truly made complete in him. This is how we know we are in him: Whoever claims to live in him must walk as Jesus did.
> (1 John 2:3-6)

> Do you not know that your bodies are members of Christ himself? Shall I then take the members of Christ and unite them with a prostitute? Never! Do you not know that he who unites himself with a prostitute is one with her in body? For it is said, "The two will become one flesh."
> (1 Corinthians 6:15-16)

spiritually, but emotionally as well. Because sexual intimacy unites two people, sexual intercourse with the wrong person can do emotional damage to us. Mike feels that because he had sex before marriage it is harder for him to really feel bonded to his wife. Kristin feels like a piece of her heart was broken to pieces by having sex with her boyfriend, who later broke up with her. Maybe sex before marriage is one reason why

> Scientific studies show that people who have had less sex before marriage are happier with their marriages, enjoy sex more in their marriages, and divorce less often than people who had more sex before they were married.

so many people now find it hard to have good marriages. By having sex with people other than our husbands or wives, we may be breaking down our ability to really unite with the person we marry. It is like bonding together with another person and then ripping apart again over and over. If the person who has had sex is really sorry and asks God to forgive and heal him or her of this damage, we believe God can and will help that person. But shouldn't we protect ourselves from this kind of damage by not having sex outside of marriage?

Look deep into your heart. Which sounds like the better life to you? Would you like to stay single all your life, perhaps having sex with five or ten or fifty people, or be married two to five times? Or would you rather have one person whom you truly love, whom you marry and stay bonded to for life, having and raising children together, and having your special partner and companion through all of life with you until you part at death? If the second type of life sounds better, then saving sex for marriage is a good idea.

But, people still will try to convince you otherwise.

1. *Sex is the very best way to express affection and love.* We've all heard it: "If you really love someone, you will have sex with that person." The truth is that sexual

intercourse *is* one of the best ways of expressing *true* love, the love that goes along with the lifelong commitment of a marriage. And the best way to find out whether the love you feel is the kind of real love that will last a lifetime is *not* to have sex before marriage. Instead, take the time to really get to know and love the person you are feeling so good about. True love, the kind on which you can build a marriage, can wait from when you both feel your love is a gift from God that means you should get married, until you actually marry each other, to have sex. You don't have to have sex to express love. You can express your love for each other by kindness, thoughtfulness, and by just enjoying all the good and wonderful things about being with the person you love.

2. *You must have sex to be a mature, normal, and grownup person.* Some people will hint that if you haven't had sex, you must still be a kid, that you must have sex to enter the world of adults. But who is really mature? The person who goes along with the crowd and believes what the television and movies tell her to believe? Or the person who believes God and the Bible, and has the strength to do what is right even when many people around him aren't? The Bible says a mature person has self-control, knows that loving and obeying God is what is really important, and is wise and strong. And a mature person doesn't need to have sex before marriage.

3. *You simply must have sex.* Here's the lie you will hear: the desire for sex is so strong that it cannot be resisted. But Jesus lived for thirty-three years on the earth, and He never had sex. Millions of Christians have lived their whole lives single and never had sex, while others have saved sex for marriage over many years. Today most of the girls who graduate from high school have had sex at least once. But just thirty years ago, less than twenty girls in every one hundred had sex by the time they graduated from high school. If we *have* to have sex, how could women (and

men) at other times have chosen not to have sex? Even today, young women in Japan and many other cultures have sex before they marry much less frequently than do young women in America. It is a lie that we *must* have sex.

4. *It's important to try sex before you get married to make sure you are "sexually compatible."* This statement means that you should try sex with different people until you find someone with whom sex is very good; then you can be more confident in marrying that person. This is terrible advice. What makes two people sexually compatible, what makes their sexual relationship full of joy and pleasure and beauty, is the quality of the love they share and their desire to please each other. There is no special, magic way two bodies fit together that makes sex great; you do not have to "shop around" by having sex with twenty people to find the "best fit." A loving married couple *creates* sexual compatibility by learning how to please each other better and better the longer they live together. Two people who truly love each other will work to improve their sexual relationship over the years of their marriage so their joy with each other can grow more and more.

5. *You need to have sex now to practice for marriage.* The idea here is that the more you have sex before marriage, the better you will be at it and the better sex will be in your marriage. But, as we just said, the couple who saves sex can have the joy of practicing and learning to love each other better after they are married. Also, scientific studies show that people who have sex with lots of people before marriage have less happy marriages, more divorces, and less happiness with sex in marriage.

6. *Sex is always good.* Do television shows and movies focus on someone getting pregnant or catching a disease after casually having sex? No. Was sex good for the thousands of people who now have sexually transmitted diseases, including HIV infection and AIDS? Was sex good for the million teenage girls every year who get pregnant? Was

it good for the half-million babies born to teenage girls who aren't married, or the other half million that are aborted by their mothers? Was it good for the girls who had sex because their boyfriends lied and claimed to love them and a month later moved on to another girl? Sexual intercourse is not always good.

Why Some Choose Sex Before Marriage

Given these reasons, why would anyone choose sex before marriage?

Some teens believe some or all of the arguments we just discussed. But there are many other reasons why people choose to have sex before marriage.

Some people have sex for the pleasure of it. Though you may not feel this way now, after puberty the thought of having sex will not sound "gross" or "yucky" anymore. It will sound like it could feel good. Is this a good reason? No. First, while sex *can* actually be pleasurable, it is not nearly as pleasurable for many teenagers as the movies and television programs suggest. For many women, especially, it takes the love and concern and sharing of marriage to make sex its best. Second, many teenagers seek the pleasure of sex because they have no purpose for their lives other than to have as much fun as possible. Their lives lack the important purposes of loving, serving, and worshiping God. So they think, *Why shouldn't I have sex if that is the best way to have a good time?* Having sex is a way to try to fill up an empty space in their lives. But only the love of Christ can fill up your life. God made sex to be a pleasure that a man and woman can gradually grow to enjoy in their marriage, not something to play around with on a date with a person you hardly know.

Some teenagers have sex because they are lonely. Girls who don't have deep friendships with their girlfriends often wind up having sex with boys. We all need friendships. Girls who don't have good friendships will often give sex to boys in order to make the boys more interested in them. It's like they are buying friendship with guys by having sex. Lonely guys also long for sex to help them feel close to someone. Having sex makes you feel close for a few minutes, but it doesn't satisfy you the way real love can. The lonely person needs the real love of some good friendships and the kind of real romantic love that waits until after marriage to have sex. Most importantly, the lonely person needs to find out how the love of God can fill his or her heart. Sex is not the medicine to heal the lonely person's hurts.

Some young women think that having a baby that depends on them and belongs only to them will make their loneliness go away. This almost always results in disaster. That baby will love its mother. But it will also change the girl's life forever, pulling her further away from friends and making it even harder to meet a man who can be her husband. The mother often winds up even more lonely. Some guys also try to "make a baby," not because they want someone to love, but because they think that you are a *real man* when you get a girl pregnant. This too usually results in disaster.

Some kids have sex because they give in to pressure. The teenage years are a time when it's very painful not to be liked by all of your "friends." If you are a teenage girl with a group of girlfriends who are having sex, you'll probably get teased and pressured to "lose your virginity." Guys can be pretty ruthless with each other. Some guys will accuse a boy who does not have sex of being homosexual or crazy or of secretly being a woman. Having sex because of pressure doesn't make anyone like you or love you more. It only proves that you don't have the strength to stand on your own to do what is right.

A special kind of pressure can come from the person you are dating. When your parents or grandparents were dating, it was almost always the man who would try to put pressure on the woman to have sex, and it was generally expected that the woman would always say no unless she was a "dirty" sort of woman or a prostitute (someone who has sex for money). Now, pressure to have sex is almost as likely to come from the girl as from the boy. Either one may ask, beg, or demand to have sex, saying things like "I just want us to be closer in our love" or "If we don't have sex I'm going to explode" or "You say you love me, but the real proof of love is making love." Some people aren't strong enough to stand up to this pressure, and so they choose to have sex.

Some people have sex because they are very insecure— they don't have a firm idea of what they believe or what kind of person they are, so they can't feel good about who they are. People who are insecure try to find ways to feel better about themselves, like having other people tell them that they are liked or that they have "passed the test." People may challenge you to prove your manhood (or womanhood) by having sex. Insecure people may do what others challenge them to do so those other people will say they're "cool" or okay. It is a terrible idea to have sex to get approval. Having sex proves nothing about you except, perhaps, that you are foolish and weak.

There are many other reasons why people have sex. Many guys want sex because it is a "conquest." It makes them feel superior to get what they want from a girl, and some guys will do anything to get that conquest. It is wrong to use another person to make yourself feel superior, especially when the way you are using that person, sex, is meant to be an act of love and unselfish giving. This, like all of the other reasons we have given for having sex outside of marriage, is not a good reason. The only good and perfect reason to have sex is to express joy and pleasure and union in marriage.

Summing It Up
Billboards, magazine covers, television shows and movies, and even "friends" will all tell you lies about sex and about what will make your life good. By saving sexual intercourse for marriage, you will be pleasing God by your obedience; you will be protecting yourself against the dangers of phys-

ical diseases, pregnancy, and emotional pain; and you will be preparing yourself to build a marriage of real unity and love. You probably feel too young to think about these things, much less to make such big decisions about your life, but you are not! Now is the right time to think and pray about these matters, and to decide which way your life will go.

CHAPTER SEVEN

LOVE AND DATING

The last time you saw a boy and girl on a date holding hands, or gazing into each other's eyes, or perhaps hugging and kissing, how did you feel about it? Did you feel, "That's disgusting; I can't imagine ever wanting to do that!" Or did you feel, "I can't wait until I can do that."

Before they go through puberty, most kids think love and dating are gross. But by the time they are fifteen or sixteen years old, love and dating sound wonderful (and maybe a little frightening). By that age, many kids have felt they were "in love" a number of times.

Part of how we feel about dating and romance is wrapped up with how we feel about other people's bodies. Before we go through puberty, most of us have a child's curiosity about other people's bodies, but after puberty we feel differently. Young men and women both find themselves attracted to certain other people. The interest in our bodies is more than just curiosity; it can include powerful feelings of excitement and desire that are strange and

unsettling. After puberty, our feelings about sexual intercourse and other ways of being physically close, like kissing, change too. What seemed gross when we were nine or
ten no longer seems that way.

What Makes Me Change My Mind?

Part of it is probably due to actual changes in the way your
brain works. The same hormones that cause your body to
mature also change your brain and the way your mind and
feelings work.

Your thinking about sex is also a result of your maturing as a person. Part of being a child is being dependent
on your parents and longing to have them protect and take
care of you. Part of being an adult, on the other hand, is
being independent and starting a family of your own. To
do that, you need to have a love relationship with one special person from outside your family. So feeling sexual desire
and love is part of the normal process of maturing and
becoming independent of your family. God wants you to
grow up and feel these things because it is part of His plan
for you as an adult.

So, what does it mean to date and who should you date?
Let's talk about that, your feelings toward people of the opposite sex, and some of the problems and challenges of dating.

It's a Date!

Many kids today start dating too early and miss wonderful
opportunities to form friendships and really get to know
other people. We want to help you get your ideas straight
about dating so you can make good choices in the years
ahead.

Here's a scene: A guy pulls into a girl's driveway in the
car he's borrowed from his parents. Maybe he honks the
horn, or maybe he goes up and rings the doorbell. The girl
comes out and they go out for the evening—to a play at
school, a football game, a dinner and a movie, or maybe

roller skating. They enjoy their time together, and the boy brings her home approximately thirty seconds before the absolute deadline her parents gave her for being home. That's what many people consider a "date" or "going out."

But dating isn't always that way. In our community some kids start "going out" in the seventh or eighth grade. The funny thing to us parents is that kids who "go out" don't actually go anywhere. "Going out" means that a boy and a girl like each other and talk together on the phone or exchange notes or talk at school.

Dating is really just an opportunity to get to know another person you particularly like. One of the best ways to get to know another person when you are fourteen or fifteen is to have that person join your group of friends in a church or school group activity. Having that person come to your youth group, join your Bible study, or go with you to something like a roller-skating party can be an opportunity to find out what kind of person he or she is without a lot of pressure or expectations.

As you grow older and start to have more definite interests in certain people, it is usually possible to spend more time with them at such activities. You can discuss with your parents the possibility of meeting this person at a school basketball game or a church event. As you get older yet and desire to spend more time with one particular person, it can be fun to "group-date" with two or three couples going on something like a hike or bike ride, to the movies, or doing a service project for your church.

Finally, you can begin to have dates when you spend special time just with this person you like. We suggest that young people not do independent "car dating" until they are at least sixteen or seventeen years old. By "car dating" we mean the kind of dating where a young man and woman are on their own to do the activities that they choose (with the permission of the parents). By waiting until you are sixteen or seventeen, you will have more confidence in your ability to take care of yourself since you are now old enough to drive and get a job. You also have waited long enough that you at least have had some experience in handling yourself in challenging situations, so if something is not right, you can take care of yourself.

Does It Matter Who I Date?

The Bible instructs us that it is not wise for a Christian to marry someone who is not a Christian. Why? Most married people discover just how important it is that both partners in the marriage look at life the same way. It adds strength to your marriage if you both believe in God, can pray together, value the same things in life, believe the same things are right and wrong, and can enjoy your involvement in serving and worshiping God together in your church. Couples who don't have a common bond of faith often find that their different views of God slowly become more painful and difficult.

> Do not be yoked together with unbelievers. For what do righteousness and wickedness have in common? Or what fellowship can light have with darkness? (2 Corinthians 6:14)

We believe it is very important for Christians to seriously date only other Christians. You can see why this makes sense: the longer you date someone, the more involved you become with that person. Sometimes you become so interested in this other person that you don't have as good judgment as you should. Be careful about continuing to date a person who does not share your faith; you may help that person's faith grow stronger, but he or she may help your faith grow weaker. And the weaker your faith, the poorer the choices you might make. If the other person is a Christian, you have a good basis on which to get to know him or her further.

He Loves Me, He Loves Me Not?

One of the most frightening, wonderful, confusing, and joyous experiences of the teenage years is falling in love.

These feelings come in so many different varieties they are hard to describe. When you are just beginning to be interested in the opposite sex, you may find yourself thinking that a certain person is especially nice. You feel like you want to do things for that person, and you want that person to be a special friend. When these feelings grow stronger, you can really feel swept away by them. Some teenagers find themselves thinking about this person all the time: daydreaming about him, night-dreaming about her, writing his name over and over, planning how to spend extra time with her.

Especially in the early teenage years, some kids love to tease and taunt others who are obviously having romantic feelings toward another person. Someone may pick on you with embarrassing questions or crude comments.

Sometimes grownups are not much better. They can be insensitive about what you feel are real love feelings. A parent might call those feelings "puppy love" or some other name that implies they aren't real. Sometimes a parent will even say, "Oh, you aren't really in love." This kind of reaction by adults is understandable because, believe it or not, your parents and all of the adults around you have had the same feelings. Most parents who see their child going through the process of being "head-over-heels-in-love" remember all the times they had similar feelings at your age, and how those relationships almost always fell apart in disappointment. This can make parents a little skeptical about your feelings.

Do you want to find out something new about your parents? Talk to them about the times they were in love when they were teenagers. Ask them to tell you how they felt, and what kind of things they did as a result of feeling like they were in love. Get them to tell you about the times they "went steady," about the silliest thing they did to express their affection, about what it felt like to be in love and also what it felt like when a relationship broke up.

While a skeptical adult reaction is understandable, it is

also unfortunate. It treats the real feelings of a teenager as if they were unimportant and mistaken. A teenager's feelings should be treated with respect and care. What you feel at that moment are real feelings, and they are precious and beautiful. God made you capable of feeling that kind of strong caring and affection, and that is a very special gift from God.

Take the Test

But even if those feelings are real and a gift from God, that still doesn't mean that the love you feel when you are thirteen or sixteen or nineteen is a mature or "true" love. There are only two tests that will show whether love is real or not. *The first is the test of time.* We remember times from our teenage years when we felt passionately, wildly, almost crazily in love with another person, and it was amazing how two weeks later we no longer had those feelings. A love that is true will stand the test of time as you get to know the other person better and better. True love finds out more of who the other person really is, and grows to appreciate more and more about that person. *The second test of true love is the test of restraint.* A love that is true will grow slowly over time as the couple acts toward each other in the way that God wants them to. Having too much of a physical relationship can actually prevent you from getting to know each other better.

There is one other thing young people should know and understand about feelings of love. They are almost always connected with the sexual feelings of our bodies. God made us so that the more feelings of love and infatuation we have, the more sexual feelings and desires we feel.

When you're a young child your feelings of love toward your family go naturally with a desire to hug and kiss and touch them. This is a way you express your love with your body. The attraction and love feelings that you have as a teenager include this desire to hug or kiss, but the feelings are different and stronger. You may have noticed that couples who seem really "in love" touch each other a lot, holding hands and putting their arms around each other. Some (but not all) moms and dads act this way toward each other; they hug and kiss their children, but the hugs and kisses and pats they give each other are different somehow from those they give their children.

God made us so that our feelings of love or attraction are connected to having sexual feelings about the person we love. When a fourteen-year-old boy thinks about the girl he has a crush on, he may find himself with an erection—a sign of sexual excitement. A fourteen-year-old girl may notice a slight wetness in her vagina when she thinks about a boy she is attracted to. These feelings do not mean that this boy or girl is thinking about sexual intercourse or even about the other person's body. It only means that God made us so that our feelings of love and interest in another person are connected with how our bodies respond sexually. This is a great gift, because later when you are fully an adult and married, your sexual relationship with your wife or husband will be a wonderful way for you to express your love. After you go through puberty, you will begin to respond to feelings of love as a whole person (body, mind, emotions, and spirit), like an adult.

As a teenager, you may find yourself thinking how wonderful the person you are in love with looks. You may like hugging and holding the other person, or thinking of being married to him or her. All of these feelings, and even the feeling that having sexual intercourse with the person would be wonderful, are part of the natural way we respond when we have feelings of love. God makes us capable of these kinds of feelings, but it is vital that we use this gift the way that God intends. Many teenagers today wrongly believe that if you have any feeling that something would be fun or exciting, you should go ahead and do it.

But just because we have feelings of wanting something

does not mean that it is right for us to have it. Our teenage feelings about sex are one good example of that. It is a good gift from God that a teenage couple in love are excited by each other, interested in each other, and that the thought of having sex is an exciting and appealing thing. But God does not want them to choose to have sex. Sexual intercourse is to be reserved for marriage. By choosing not to have sex, a couple can take the time to really grow to know each other and have a clear sense of whether this is the person God wants them to marry. Having sex with a person you are not married to hurts you and hurts the relationship you will someday have with your husband or wife. It also hurts God, because having sex outside of marriage is disobedient to God's command and a signal to Him that we do not love Him with our whole heart.

To Touch Or Not to Touch

Okay, we know that sexual intercourse is something we are not supposed to do before marriage. Are there ways that people can express affection or "be sexual" in dating that are okay in God's eyes?

This is a difficult question, partly because it's embarrassing to talk about. But it's also hard because the Bible doesn't talk directly about these things. Is that because God doesn't care what we do as long as we don't have sexual intercourse? We believe the answer to that question is no. God cares very much what we do even when we are not having sexual intercourse.

"Dating" as we know it did not exist in the times the Bible was written. Most people lived in very small towns and villages. Even the large cities of ancient Palestine were small by today's standards. Marriages were arranged, which means that parents would make the decision about who their children would marry. It was not uncommon for children to grow up knowing who they were going to marry. People would often marry young, almost always before they were twenty. Couples would not often be left alone because it was important that they not have sex before they were married. They had none of the privacy young couples have today where they can hop in a car and drive twenty or thirty miles away from anyone who knows them. In that ancient culture God didn't need to speak of rules for how people should behave when they dated, because they didn't date. Often they only got to know each other after they were married.

To think this through, we have to be clear about what we are talking about. Human beings have been very creative in what they do for sexual excitement and to make their bodies feel good sexually. Even a simple touch on the shoulder or pat on the back can feel exciting if the person who touches you is someone you like or love. A couple might hold hands or put their arms around each other. It's very common for couples to kiss when they have feelings of love for each other. But there are kisses and then there are *kisses*. A kiss may be a very simple peck on the cheek or the lips. Or, instead of a quick peck, the couple may kiss with their lips for a little bit longer. And then there is passionate kissing that you have probably seen on television or in a movie when the couple seems stuck together for minutes. This kind of kissing is called "French" or "deep" kissing: the couple open their lips and touch their tongues together as well as their lips. (We don't know of a single child who, when he or she first hears of this, doesn't say, "That is the most disgusting thing I've ever heard; I will *never* do that!") Our advice is to save your kisses for a very special person, and don't get involved at all in what we are about to discuss.

In spite of what the movies and television programs show, most couples do not go directly from passionate kissing to having sexual intercourse. Some couples who are very attracted to each other gradually share more and more of their bodies with each other without having sexual intercourse. When couples are feeling strong feelings of love, it is natural to want to touch the other person's body, even his or her private parts—the woman's breasts and both partners' genitals. When teenagers let the other person touch their private parts or when they touch the other person's private parts, they are doing something that is much more intimate than just kissing. The intimacy gets even greater if the couple begins to unbutton or take off their clothes so they are even sharing more of their bodies. Instead of touching the other person through their clothes, they may directly touch the other person's uncovered breasts or genitals. These and the many other ways in which people touch each other without having sexual intercourse are called "petting." This is an awkward name. We usually think of petting pets, not people. As you listen to other kids talk you may hear other slang words that mean the same thing as petting.

What does God think of petting? As we said already, the Bible doesn't give any direct rules about petting. But in Matthew 5:27-30, Jesus talks with great seriousness about the problem of "lust." He emphasizes that the Bible speaks against people having sex with someone they are not married to. Then He goes on to say, "But I tell you that anyone who looks at a woman lustfully has already committed adultery with her in his heart." By this, Jesus seems to mean that what we do with our thoughts and in our hearts is just as important as what we do with our bodies. We should do more than just keep our bodies from doing things that break God's rules; we should also try not to have desires or thoughts about breaking God's rules. These words of Jesus suggest that it is very unwise for teenage couples to engage in petting. When a couple begins petting, they are encouraging their hearts and minds to think about sex more and more. This can lead them into exactly the kind of lustful thoughts that Jesus was speaking against.

Also, the reason the Bible tells us not to have sexual intercourse with someone we are not married to is to protect us against being bonded or glued to someone we are not married to. Sexual intercourse provides that special kind of bonding. But people who engage in petting often experience some of this kind of bonding because they are sharing much of their bodies openly with another person. In sexual intercourse you share all of your body with the other person. But in petting you *begin* the process of sharing your body.

Lastly, petting can be dangerous simply because people who do it often get very sexually excited, and when they are excited they do not make good decisions. A teenager may feel very confident that she should not do petting or have intercourse. But if she starts some petting with her boyfriend, she may find herself thinking, *This is so exciting that I bet I can handle a bit more . . . and a bit more than that. . . .* Many teens who wind up having sexual intercourse were not planning to do that before they got going in petting. So petting can be dangerous because it can cause you to make bad decisions.

The reason we wanted to tell you about these things is so that you can think about them and make a decision about what you will and will not do before you even start developing a close relationship with another person. We urge you to decide now that you will be careful with the precious gift of your sexual body. By choosing not to have sexual intercourse with anyone before you marry, and by choosing to keep your body private and special by not petting, you are honoring God. You are making the gift of your body to the person that you may marry someday that much more special. If you stay single, you are protecting yourself from possible problems and are giving the gift of your body to God, just like He wants (Romans 12:1-2).

Some Really Good Advice About Dating

☞ Keep your other friendships going while dating; don't depend on dating as your only kind of friendship.

☞ Don't start dating too early. You have plenty of time to learn about love, so take your time.

☞ Ease gradually into dating as you are ready and as your parents agree you are ready.

☞ Relax. Enjoy a friendship rather than pursue your possible spouse.

☞ Date only Christians. Your companions will affect who you are.

☞ Be accountable to your parents for definite plans for dates. Do what you say you will do.

☞ When on a date, avoid movies and television programs that focus on sex or that aim to get viewers sexually excited.

☞ Dress modestly for a date. Don't send out mixed signals.

☞ Be prepared to talk openly about your moral standards about sex with the person you are dating.

☞ Include prayer in dating, perhaps before and after a date.

☞ Include the person you date in the important parts of your life, like family gatherings and at church.

CHAPTER EIGHT

TOUGH ANSWERS TO SOME TOUGH PROBLEMS

▼

What if my date tries to force me to have sex? What if my best friend is having sex with her boyfriend? Couldn't living together before marriage prepare a couple for the real thing? What do I do if my sex-education teacher gives advice I don't agree with? Is masturbation evil? My friend thinks he might be "gay"—now what do I do? How can I believe in marriage when my parents couldn't make it work?

As a young person trying to live a life that is pleasing to God, you will face some tough issues. We wish you would not have to face any of the issues we will discuss in this chapter, but maybe our words will help you make good decisions before you do face them, or be a better friend to someone who is dealing with these problems.

Negative Attitudes Toward Women

People who observe how girls develop into women have noticed a very disturbing pattern that may be happening to you or your friends. In the elementary school years girls do just as well as boys in school. They feel just as good about themselves and speak up and express their opinions just as freely as boys do. But in the middle school years many girls lose their confidence. They stop thinking of themselves as capable and become full of doubt and insecurity.

Nobody quite knows why this happens to so many young women. It may be that some teachers begin to direct most of their attention to the boys in a class, and the girls may be treated as if they were not there. Also, middle school boys begin to respond with excitement and appreciation to girls, but often only to the girls they think are attractive and don't act smart and confident. Girls who don't look exactly like fashion models begin to feel left out, and girls who ought to take pride in their musical skills, their athletic abilities, their intelligence and capabilities in schoolwork often feel they don't matter.

There *are* many good things happening for women today, especially in America. Women are able to get more education than ever before. It's becoming more and more common for women to be scientists, doctors, political leaders, lawyers, and business people. Fewer women today die in childbirth.

But women continue to be physically abused in their marriages—beaten up by their husbands. Women are treated as sex objects in the media, as having value only for their bodies. The message seems to be: "If you look right, you matter. If not, forget it." And there is a lot of confusion today about what a woman *should* do with her life—career, marriage and motherhood, or both?

What can we do about all of this? All of us need to think about women and men the way God does. The first truth we have in the Bible about men and women is that they were created equally in the image of God.

So God created man in his own image,
   in the image of God he created him;
   male and female he created them. (Genesis 1:27)

The Apostle Paul picks up this same idea in Galatians 3:28 where he says, "There is neither Jew nor Greek, slave nor free, male nor female, for you are all one in Christ Jesus."

Women cannot be worth less than men or treated as objects because they are created in the image of God. And we need to act on that belief. Girls need to act in confidence that they are just as loved by and special to God as are boys. Boys who are reading this chapter should remember to treat girls with respect. In the words of Jesus, boys should "do to others what you would have them do to you."

The Challenge of Pressure from Your Friends

When Blake was in seventh grade, he hung out with a rough group of guys in his neighborhood. One day these friends shoplifted candy from a convenience store and then teased and harassed Blake because he didn't steal anything. Blake knew it wasn't right, but he caved in to their pressure. Next time they went to that store he also stole, and did so again several times over the next few weeks. Finally he realized that he did not want to grow up being a thief. It was painful to choose to stop hanging around with that group of friends and put up with their name-calling and pressure. That was his first powerful experience of pressure from friends.

Part of being a teenager is wanting to fit in with your friends. In the teen years you are becoming your own person. Having close friends during these years keeps you from feeling so glued to your family and gives you a sense of being a different and unique person. You are no longer just a child in your family; you are now your own person. But how do you make sure that you really are your own person and not just someone who does whatever your peer group tells you to do?

Teenagers are often pressured to use cigarettes, alcohol, and drugs, even though people who do these things are more likely to experiment with sex, or do poorly in school, or even be in trouble with the police. Steve gets teased at school for being a virgin. Cindy gets pressure on a date to have sex. How can you handle it when people put pressure on you to have sex or use alcohol? How do you stand up for the truth when it hurts for others to make fun of you?

First, we are always weakest when we stand alone. All of us feel stronger when we know others who agree with us. Of course, we are not really alone if we are doing what is right, because Jesus stands with us. With God on our side, we are a match for anything. "If God is for us, who can be against us?" (Romans 8:31). But even when Christ is for us, it helps to have another person beside us. That's the reason it's so important to be part of a youth group from your church or a Christian group that prays together or studies the Bible at school. You will be more able to stand up to the pressure of other kids when you know you have friends who believe as you do.

> I have set before you life and death, blessings and curses. Now choose life, so that you and your children may live and that you may love the LORD your God, listen to his voice, and hold fast to him. (Deuteronomy 30:19-20)

Second, handling pressure successfully starts with deciding what you will and will not do. Decide now whether or not you will have sex before you are married. Don't wait until you are out on a date or at someone's house to decide. Think through what we have said in this book. Talk with God about your decision. If you believe that we have been telling you the truth about sex, *make that decision right now.*

> Choose for yourselves this day whom you will serve. . . . But as for me and my household, we will serve the LORD. (Joshua 24:15)

After you make a decision, tell God, your parents, and a Christian friend about that decision. It pleases God when

His people make and keep promises to Him.

Third, think through how you will handle pressure. Most of this pressure will come in the form of comments like: "What's the matter with you; are you a prude?" "Haven't you grown up yet, or are you still a child?" "What are you, gay or something; don't you have normal sexual desires?" "But we have got to have sex or I'm going to go crazy!" "You say that you care for me but you don't show it by doing what people who love each other do." "If you don't have sex with me I'm going to ruin your reputation all over school by telling everyone what a prude and virgin you are!" "Please, if we just do it this one time I won't ask again." "You said you'd go out with me, and that means that you would have sex, so stop being a tease!"

It is not important that you have a snappy, clever answer to any of these comments. It is important that you say no *forcefully* in a way that indicates you really mean it. You do not have to reason or have a long discussion with the person pressuring you. You can simply say, "I do not choose to have sex with you (or kiss you or let you touch me). I want to go home now, and so our date is over." If someone is putting a lot of pressure on you and won't stop, you may have to promise that you'll complain about the person's behavior to your parents, the person's parents, a school counselor, or some authority figure.

Pressure to have sex can sometimes get even worse. A number of girls report being forced to have sex on a date. Sometimes a girl may let herself be talked into having sex, or she may feel threatened by a boy who says he'll ruin her reputation at school. Young women need to be strong to handle these kinds of threats if they occur. No one has the right to force you to do anything you don't want to do. Most people who make threats cannot carry them out, but if they actually do, the things they threatened are not nearly as bad as having sex would have been. You must decide what you will and will not do, and then be ready to fight, both with your words and with your body.

If a person uses threats against you, you should demand to be taken home right then and promise to report anything that happens to your parents, the police, the boy's parents, and any other appropriate authority. In extreme cases, you may have to be prepared to fight back physically. God does not want you to be a victim. A slap, a poke in the eye, twisting a finger until it breaks—all of these seem like extreme actions, but they may help you get out of a situation that is out of control and help you preserve your own safety. We know it is scary to talk about these things, but by having a clear idea about what you should and shouldn't do, you can protect yourself and keep yourself safe. And the best thing you can do about this kind of situation is to prevent it from ever happening by knowing well the person you are with, making it clear what your standards are, being sure he is a Christian, and having safe plans for your time together.

When a Friend Is Having Sex

One of the hardest things for teens to handle is when a friend reveals to you that he or she is having sex. Robert had counted on Travis as a friend who was committed to saving sex for marriage. Melissa felt that Rachel would always be there to help her stay strong in living her sexuality God's way. But Robert and Melissa, both seventeen, found that their respective friends had begun having sex with the person they were dating. Travis told Robert that he and his girlfriend still both believed sex outside of marriage was wrong, but that they somehow found themselves going "too far" and couldn't seem to stop. Rachel told Melissa that she had changed her mind. She was sure she was in love with her boyfriend, and it just didn't seem wrong to give her body to him when she loved him so much.

This could happen to you. How would you handle it? Every situation is different, and there is no one answer. You must balance two very difficult truths: your friend needs your help, but having a friend who is having sex may tempt you to have sex as well.

Your friend needs your gentleness, your help, to get him back on the right path. Maybe you can help her see that her boyfriend has been putting pressure on her. Maybe you can help him resist the temptation to have sex. You can gently remind her that sex outside of marriage is a sin that hurts God and hurts the person, and that God's gift of sex is too precious to use wrongly.

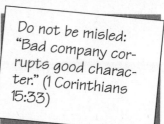

If someone is caught in a sin, you who are spiritual should restore him gently. But watch yourself, or you also may be tempted. (Galatians 6:1)

Do not be misled: "Bad company corrupts good character." (1 Corinthians 15:33)

But you also have to realize that you are in danger of being tempted. When you talk about sex with your friend, your talk may be helping your friend, or it might be hurting you. Kids who have sex often feel guilty, and one way to make that guilt go away is to convince themselves *and their friends* that sex outside of marriage is okay. You may think you are helping your friend, but he or she may be trying to get you to change your mind. So try to help, but be honest enough to know that you can only help so much. And pray hard about your friend and for yourself in this situation. When you feel that nothing is changing or that your own beliefs are weakening, that is the time to say, "This friendship is hurting me and my relationship with God. I need to back off and just pray for my friend." And don't try to help all alone. Make sure you have friends who are helping you stay strong in what you believe.

What About Pornography?
Pornography means any magazine, video, movie, book, or picture that shows or discusses people having sex or the

private parts of the human body in a way designed to sexually arouse people in an unwholesome way. You may have already heard of "dirty magazines" or about movies that have very explicit "sex scenes" in them. Now there are even pornographic programs on computers!

Looking at pornography can be very appealing to teenagers, especially to teenage boys (since most pornography is about women's bodies). All of us are curious about the human body and about sex. Pornographic pictures are made in such a way as to make the person who looks at them get sexually excited. A person might think, *Well, it's not like I'm having sex with anyone, and this isn't hurting anyone else. I'm finding out about sex, and it seems exciting to me. What could be wrong with this?*

Is there anything really wrong with pornography? The decisions you make as a teenager will shape the kind of adult you become. Like petting, the Bible doesn't talk directly about pornography. But there are many things in the Bible that suggest that it is not a good thing to look at it.

☞ The Bible suggests that who you are sexually is meant to be private, shared only with the person you marry someday. But in pornography, people are sharing their bodies with thousands of other people. Taking pictures of a sexual relationship and making them available to others violates the privacy of sex.

☞ The Bible says lust is wrong, and Jesus said lust is committing adultery with another person in your heart. When people look at pornography, often it encourages them to think about having sex with the person in the pictures. By looking at pornography, you are encouraging yourself to lust.

☞ By looking at pornography, you are filling your mind with images of how sex should be. These images are almost all false. Pornography usually presents sex as selfish men think it should be, rather than in the beautiful, sharing, giving way God meant it to be.

For all of these reasons, protect your mind and heart by staying away from pornography. The teenager who uses pornography is training his mind to move away from what God wants.

Living Together

Many people today live together before they are married. This is called **cohabitation**. Some people think, *There is so much divorce. It makes sense to live together before you get married. It's like a trial marriage. Living together gives you a chance to get to know the other person, to make a better decision about whether you want to get married, and to make sure sex with the other person will be good.*

This view is wrong. Cohabitation is wrong first because God does not want people to have sex outside of marriage. Sex is to be reserved for marriage, not to experiment with before marriage. Second, scientists have been studying the effects of cohabitation for years, and every scientific study agrees: people who cohabit before they marry have *more problems and less happiness* with their marriage and sexual relationship, and a *higher divorce rate*, than those who don't. So if you want a happy marriage, living together before marriage will not help you.

Public School Sex Education

There are many useful things you can learn in public school sex-education classes. They can give you good information about the biological aspects of sex, including more information about your body than we have covered in this book. Sex-education classes can also be an opportunity to find out what your peers in school think about sex.

But sex-education classes can be very discouraging to Christian teenagers. Some teachers assume that most of the kids in the class will be having sex. They may say once or twice that it's good not to have sex before marriage, but then the majority of the time might be spent in a way that assumes all the kids in the class will be having sex and what they need to study is how to prevent pregnancy and disease when they do have sex. If you are a Christian teenager who is seriously committed to living your sexual life God's way, this can be very discouraging. It can leave you feeling like you are the only one who is deciding to save sex for marriage.

Also, discussions about reasons for not having sex can be a problem. Some teachers and students do not respect Christian beliefs. In a sex-education class, Justin expressed his belief that God wants sex to be saved for marriage. Instead of this belief being accepted and encouraged, he was attacked for being "bossy" and "judgmental," for saying something that made other people feel guilty. Sometimes when a teenager expresses his or her belief about God's view of sex, teachers turn that view around and make it seem like the real reason the teen chooses not to have sex is because of fear of sex or a negative view about sex. Teens sometimes hear something like this: "It sounds like you are really afraid of sex. Maybe your family taught that sex is a bad, dirty, and disgusting thing. But many people don't think it is. Why do you have such negative views of sex?" It can be very upsetting to be put on the spot like this in front of classmates.

Sometimes in discussions about different moral positions, Christian kids are asked to role-play as if they believe the opposite of their own views. Teachers will say this is to help you think through all the options before you make up your mind. But it is risky to pretend in a role play that you believe sex outside marriage is okay. It is good for us to think through what we believe and to compare it to other beliefs. But God doesn't tell us to pretend to have other beliefs. God wants us to remain faithful at all times. You may ask to be excused.

Sexual Abuse —

If this has happened to you, take immediate steps to protect yourself and make the abuse stop. First, talk to your parents, particularly your mother. Mothers often have a hard time believing such a thing is happening in their family, so you need to be prepared to calmly describe what has happened and that you are not making up what you are saying. If for some reason you can't talk to a parent, then talk to your doctor, your pastor, or a school counselor. The top priority is for you to get protection. God oes not want this to happen to you.

After the abuse has stopped, it is important to get help emotional healing from the abuse. Healing of all the bad ngs and memories can be difficult; it's very important you have someone you trust to talk with about this. nen who go through this kind of experience often hate t idea of sex, hate and fear men, and have doubts about G and about ever marrying. Many young women who are ab ed feel horrible about themselves. They feel angry at the wn bodies, they feel terrible about themselves for not bein ble to stop the abuse, and they feel it must be their fault. t abuse is not their fault. If you have been abused and s ebody has told you it was your fault, don't believe that p n. Your body is not bad, sex is not bad, and all men ai ot bad. We urge you to talk to someone, to pray to God, l to give yourself time to heal.

What If Parents Did Not Handle
Their Se ity Rightly?

The most nt reason parents give us for being uncomfortable ta vith their kids about sex is that they are not proud c they handled their sexuality before they got married, as having sex or living together. Many of these parent e not Christians when they acted this way, but some m were. All of them are nervous about talking with th s about sex because a kid might ask, "Mom and Dad have sex before marriage?" Parents worry that giving an honest answer may seem like giving permission to a child to behave just as they did. And yet, parents don't want to lie to their children. So, many parents avoid the subject of sex in hopes that their own past will not come up.

How should you feel about your mom or dad's past? The truth is you do not need to repeat the past mistakes of your parents. In fact, you have the opportunity to make better decisions than they did and so experience more of the joy and blessing of God's gift of sexuality than they. As we talk to our children about life, our hope is that they will see our weaknesses, but not use those weaknesses as excuses to have the same ones. We hope each one of our children will make better decisions than we have and live a better life than we did as a result. Nothing could make us happier.

If your parents are willing to talk about their past, talk with them. We tell parents not to explain to their kids any of the details of their sexual past, but to talk with their kids about how they feel about it now that they have grown as Christians to discover more of what God meant a marriage to be. Most Christian parents who have broken God's rules about sex are able to tell their kids about the pain, suffering, and difficulty caused by their choices.

Broken Families

Lots of Christian kids grow up in homes that have been shattered by divorce, separation, or death. Many of you reading this book may live in a family where there is only one parent in the home. Many of you may live in "blended" families created by a second or third marriage. Kids suffer a lot when their family breaks up and often blame themselves for the breakup. Some kids feel a responsibility to try to get their mother and father back together. Kids feel lonely for the parent that is not there. Blended families have problems of their own: how to develop positive feelings for this stranger that is now a parent, how to get close to siblings that you don't know well, and getting used to a new location are just a few examples.

Living in a broken family can make it hard for a young person to think correctly about sex. Kids often do best when they have a parent of both sexes present to talk to. It is important for girls to be able to understand a man's perspective on sexuality, and it's natural to talk to your father about this. Similarly, boys can benefit from talking to their moms about a woman's perspective. But if these parents aren't available, ask the parent you live with who would be a good person for you to talk to.

What if your feelings about marriage have been soured by seeing your parents go through a messy divorce? Some of you may be thinking, *Well, I'm a Christian, and I'll follow God's rules about sex, but I don't ever plan to be married because I know how awful that can be.* Sadly, many marriages are painful. But marriage is still a gift from God, and when a marriage is good, it is a tremendous blessing. Don't give up on marriage. But every marriage involves struggle and sacrifice. For those of us who have good marriages, the joy and blessing we receive is well worth all the struggle and sacrifice. Look around for Christian marriages that really do represent the goodness that God intends in marriage. These marriages can be a sign to you of the good that is possible.

If you are in a single-parent family where your parent works so hard to provide all the support for the kids that she or he doesn't have much energy to talk with you, or go to your school activities, or support you in other ways, this can leave you feeling on your own. If you have these feelings, talk with your parent about what might be done. It can help to develop Christian friendships through your church or school that can help you stay strong and make the right decisions. You may even be able to get close to the parents of some of your friends.

Homosexuality

A **homosexual** is a person who feels sexual desire for people of the same sex (a man for a man, a woman for a woman) and feels little sexual desire for a person of the opposite sex. The word *gay* is used for men who are homosexuals, and the word *lesbian* is used for women who are homosexuals. How should we think about homosexuality? This is a big and complicated area, but here are a few guidelines.

First, homosexuals are people, and they deserve to be treated as people. People who are not homosexual have caused a lot of suffering for gay men and lesbian women. We have made it almost impossible for young people who are trying to figure out their sexual feelings to talk about these kinds of feelings without living in fear of ridicule. People make cruel jokes about gays and lesbians, they spout off feelings of hatred when they don't even know homosexual people. No one, especially Christians, should hate homosexual people.

But, the Bible does condemn homosexual behavior. It calls homosexual behavior "detestable" and immoral (read Leviticus 18:22 and 20:13, Romans 1:27, and 1 Corinthians 6:9). So how should we feel about homosexuals? We should feel the same way we feel toward people who have sex outside of marriage, or who commit adultery, theft, or any other sin. We should recognize they are children of God, created in God's image and loved by Him, but that God is saddened by and hates what they do.

But what does this have to do with you? We live in a time when gays and lesbians are fighting for their way of life to be recognized by the church and all of society as a valid "alternative lifestyle." There is a growing push to help young people accept and explore their homosexual feelings, even in high school or earlier. Some schools are developing "gay and lesbian support groups" that aim to "help" a young person discover and accept those feelings within himself or herself.

The major problem with this is that many of us go through a period when our sexual feelings are confusing, uncertain, and troubling. Many boys feel very strong sexual desire and find themselves having an erection without any clear understanding of what has them excited. Many boys and girls have dreams of hugging or kissing someone without a clue as to who the person was, or even if it was a man or a woman. Girls often have such strong feelings of love for their girlfriends that they wonder if those are sexual feelings and whether they might be a lesbian. As we go through puberty, we have a lot of curiosity about the bodies of the opposite sex, but also about the bodies of people of the same sex. For instance, in a locker room a boy might look around to see how other boys are developing. But if he is caught looking around, other boys may call him awful names like "fag" (a very harsh and unloving name for a homosexual man) and may tease him about that. He may even wonder if this might be true about him.

If our society moves to more and more acceptance of homosexual behavior, this might lead more young people to be confused about whether the feelings they have are those of a homosexual. You see, homosexual feelings are not something that only lifelong homosexuals have; people who wind up being heterosexual can have them too, though they don't feel them as often or as strongly. Another problem with the growing acceptance of homosexuality as a lifestyle is that it might lead more young people to experiment with homosexual behavior to see if that is their orientation. We have known people who got involved in homosexual practice while they were teenagers, sometimes with kids their own age, sometimes with slightly older kids, and sometimes with adults. The occurrence of this may well increase as homosexual practice becomes more accepted in our culture.

Christian young people need to know how to love and accept homosexual persons, but not accept their actions.

God does not approve of homosexual behavior. We need to flee from all forms of sexual immorality, and that includes homosexual behavior. Do not let the growing acceptance of homosexual behavior draw you into experimenting with homosexual sex.

If you do have occasional homosexual feelings as you go through the teenage years, this is generally nothing to worry about. It is part of the normal range of feelings that go along with growing up. If you find these feelings are very strong and you don't have any feelings of attraction toward people of the opposite sex, then you may want to talk to someone you trust about it.

CHAPTER NINE

WHAT KIND OF PERSON SHOULD I BECOME?

▼

You stand at the very edge of young adulthood. For many of you, a lot of what we've been talking about seems pretty far in the future. But some kids begin having sex as early as age thirteen or even earlier. By the time you are in seventh or eighth grade, some of you will already know of kids who are having sex, getting pregnant, getting an abortion, and having a baby. The future is almost here. As your body goes through the changes we have described, God is preparing you physically to be a mature sexual person. But becoming an adult is more than body changes.

Up until now, your parents have had a very strong influence on your life. Part of being a baby is being completely dependent on your parents for everything, of being under their control. As you go through elementary school, you slowly begin the process of becoming independent from your parents. You develop more of a mind of your own as you spend time away from them and get a better sense of how other people look at things.

Over the next five to ten years you will become your own person. Growing up means making bigger and more important decisions, and this can make the process pretty scary. If you don't realize it already, it's time for you to understand a very important truth: *You are responsible for the kind of person you become.* It's *your* decisions and choices that determine what kind of person you are and will be. Your parents and friends will still have an influence on you, but it is *your* decisions that will shape your life.

"The Devil Made Me Do It!"

Are you ever around people who talk as if they never make any choices? They don't say, "I did it because I thought that was the best thing to do" or "I did it because that is what I believed was right." Instead, they say things like "He made me do it!" or "I had to do it because of what she said" or "I had to do it or my friends wouldn't like me anymore." This kind of thinking puts all the responsibility for choices on someone else. It says other people *make* them do things.

But that doesn't change the truth that you are responsible for the kind of person you become. If you helped a kid cheat on a test because she wanted you to, she didn't make you do it. You *chose* to do it because you wanted her to like you. If you look at a pornographic magazine so the guys will stop making fun of you, they didn't make you do it. You *chose* to do it because you didn't like them making fun of you. You need to develop the habit of seeing how *you* are responsible for the decisions you make. Learn to think, *I choose to do it,* rather than, *I have to do it.* Why? Because people who understand that they make the choices actually make better decisions.

Small Is Big

You see, you are the one who is responsible for what kind of person you become. And small choices are just as important as big ones! To grow into a truthful adult, you need to make small decisions to tell the truth every day in the small areas that don't seem to matter so much (like whether you ate all your lunch, whether you got your homework done, what you did with your friends when you were gone for two hours). Sadly, kids who make bad decision after bad decision in the small areas tend later to make really big bad decisions when the pressure is on.

What seem like small, unimportant decisions make a difference in the area of sex as well. Whether you are a mature sexual person as an adult will depend on the kinds of small and big decisions you make in the next few years of your life. Deciding whether you will repeat or listen to dirty jokes today, or watch that dirty movie at a friend's house, or experiment with kissing at age twelve—these kinds of decisions are as important as the big decisions you will face later, because they all add together to make you who you are.

If the choices you make are so important, what can you do to help make the best choices? What are some good choices you can make now?

Most importantly, remember that nothing is more crucial than growing in your faith. Even as a young person, you need to decide whether you believe the truth of the Christian faith. You need to decide now who is going to be your number-one commitment in life, yourself or God. And once you've decided to make God number one, having a mature faith is not something that just happens to you. It is something you work at all of your life. Faith is like a race, and the race

> I press on to take hold of that for which Christ Jesus took hold of me. Brothers, I do not consider myself yet to have taken hold of it. But one thing I do: Forgetting what is behind and straining toward what is ahead, I press on toward the goal to win the prize for which God has called me heavenward in Christ Jesus. All of us who are mature should take such a view of things. (Philippians 3:12-15)

is won by those who have the diligence and strength to keep going, to keep pressing on.

Growing with God

So how do you keep going and grow in your faith?

One thing you can do is to make prayer an important part of your life. Prayer is asking things of God, but it is much more than that. Prayer is setting aside time to meet with God, getting quiet and allowing God to speak to us. It's a time to be honest with God and ask Him to point out what is good about our lives, and what needs changing. It's a time to ask God to forgive us for our wrong choices and actions, and to thank Him for forgiving us because Christ died on the cross for us.

It's important to take some time every day by ourselves (maybe in the morning or at night) to talk to God and listen to Him as well. And we can pray short prayers all day about whatever is on our mind, like, "Lord, please help me to be strong and to forgive that bully who always picks on me in this class."

It's also important to read the Bible. The Bible is God's Word. It is God speaking through human writers to tell us about Himself. Someone once described the Bible as a collection of God's love letters to His children. If you don't have a version of the Bible that is written for someone your age, ask your parents to buy you one. If they can't do this, save up your money and buy a copy yourself. Ask a Christian bookstore worker which type of Bible is best for a kid your age. Read it regularly, and God will speak to you. Start with a book like John, Matthew, or Romans and read a section or chapter each day. Think hard to figure out what it means; pray for God to speak to you.

It's hard to be a growing Christian all on your own. So, it's important that you attend a Bible-believing church where people are excited about their relationship with God. Participate in Bible studies and other activities. Get to know older Christian people who can teach you about growing up strong and true. Get to know a group of other Christian young people, because nothing is more encouraging than having others around who believe the way you do.

Obey what God asks you to do. The Bible says that when we don't obey God, our faith grows weak and dies. When we obey God, we get stronger. This book has been about how to obey God with your sexuality as you enter your teenage years. This is very important. But you need to obey God in all areas of your life, including your attitudes, your relationships with your parents, and how you behave with your friends. Even those who try hard to obey sometimes fail. When you fail, tell God what you have done, because God will forgive you and make you stronger because you were honest with Him. (Check out 1 John 1:9.)

> And this is my prayer: that your love may abound more and more in knowledge and depth of insight, so that you may be able to discern what is best and may be pure and blameless until the day of Christ, filled with the fruit of righteousness that comes through Jesus Christ—to the glory and praise of God. (Philippians 1:9-11)

Finally, learn to pay close attention to the consequences of all your choices. Remember that as you grow into an adult you need to be taking responsibility both for what you choose to do and for the consequences of what you choose to do.

Welcome to the first stages of adulthood! Being an adult can be great, but how your life turns out rests mostly on your shoulders—on the decisions you make about how you will live your life. Thankfully, God wants to be right there with you to help as you make those decisions, giving you His truth and strength, and filling your heart with His love and forgiveness. Sexuality is a wonderful part of God's design for your life. But it is up to you whether this gift will wind up as a blessing or a curse. Our prayer for you is that you will use this gift as God intends, and that you will be able to celebrate with joy the blessings that flow from your sexuality.

AUTHORS

Stanton L. Jones, Ph.D., is professor and chairperson of the Department of Psychology at Wheaton College, where he has been directing the development of the college's doctoral program in clinical psychology. He coauthored *Modern Psychotherapies: A Comprehensive Christian Appraisal* with Richard E. Butman, and edited *Psychology and the Christian Faith: An Introductory Reader.* He has contributed a number of articles to professional journals and to magazines such as *Christianity Today.*

Brenna B. Jones is a mother whose goals have focused on the nurture and formation of the character of her children. Her undergraduate studies were in landscape architecture at Texas A & M University. She has served as a leader in a Bible study ministry with women for a number of years.

Brenna and Stan are active in a church ministry to engaged couples. They make their home in Wheaton, Illinios, where they parent three children: Jenny, Brandon, and Lindsay.

Be sure to check out the other books
in the God's Design for Sex series.

The Story of Me

Designed for children ages three to five, *The Story of Me* lays a spiritual foundation for helping your children understand their sexuality. It identifies proper names for body parts and presents the family as God's intended framework for the nurture and love of children.
Stan and Brenna Jones   0-89109-843-7

Before I Was Born

Designed for children ages five to eight, *Before I Was Born* explains the basic nature of sexual intercourse between a husband and wife and discusses conception, fetal development, childbirth, and breast-feeding in age-appropriate language.
Carolyn Nystrom   0-89109-844-5

What's the Big Deal?

Written for children ages eight to eleven, *What's the Big Deal?* helps kids find answers to their questions about sex. It explains the basic facts about sex, why God made adults so they want to have sex, what God says about sex in the Bible, and how to respond when faced with sexual pressure from peers, TV, movies, and magazines.
Stan and Brenna Jones   0-89109-845-3

Here's practical help for telling your kids about sex.

How and When to Tell Your Kids About Sex

Telling your kids about sex doesn't have to include a nervous talk about the birds and the bees. Learn how to talk confidently with your kids about sex.
Stan and Brenna Jones   0-89109-751-1

To order copies, visit your local Christian bookstore,
call NavPress at 1-800-366-7788, or log on to www.navpress.com.

To locate a Christian bookstore near you,
call 1-800-991-7747.

NAVPRESS ®
BRINGING TRUTH TO LIFE
www.navpress.com

More great parenting resources from NavPress and Piñon Press.

Becoming the Parent God Wants You to Be

Written by best-selling author Dr. Kevin Leman, *Becoming the Parent God Wants You to Be* is a real-life parenting curriculum that helps you discover you can be a great parent—without being perfect!
Dr. Kevin Leman   1-57683-100-0

Taming the Family Zoo

Does your house sometimes feel more like a zoo than a home? *Taming the Family Zoo* will help you identify the unique personality type for each of your children and learn ways to adapt your parenting style for each child.
Jim and Suzette Brawner   1-57683-058-6

Parenting with Love and Logic

Need help with your kids? Learn how to parent with love and logic and be amazed at the great results!
Foster Cline, M.D., and Jim Fay   0-89109-311-7

Parenting Teens with Love and Logic

You don't have to dread the teenage years! Learn how to parent your teens without nagging or yelling, and prepare them for a responsible adulthood.
Foster Cline, M.D., and Jim Fay   0-89109-695-7

Raising Adults

Jim Hancock challenges assumptions and creates common ground, helping parents give their children the tools to accept responsibility and gain an adult perspective on life.
Jim Hancock   1-57683-139-6

To order copies, visit your local Christian bookstore,
call NavPress at 1-800-366-7788, or log on to www.navpress.com.

To locate a Christian bookstore near you,
call 1-800-991-7747.

NAVPRESS
BRINGING TRUTH TO LIFE
www.navpress.com